DOWNRIGHT UPRIGHT

A HISTORY OF THE CANADIAN PIANO INDUSTRY

INCLUDES BUYER'S GUIDE AND CANADIAN PIANO SERIAL NUMBERS

WAYNE KELLY

NATURAL HERITAGE/NATURAL HISTORY INC.

For my sisters,
Sharon, Nancy, and Pat

Downright Upright
Published by Natural Heritage/Natural History Inc.
P.O. Box 69, Station H
Toronto, Ontario M4C 5H7
Tel: (416) 694-7907. Fax:(416) 690-6958
Copyright ©August 1991, Wayne Kelly
All Rights Reserved

No portion of this book, with the exception of brief extracts for the purpose of literary review, may be reproduced in any form without the permission of the publishers.

Editor: Curtis Fahey
Design: Derek Chung Tiam Fook
Printed and bound in Canada by Hignell Printing Limited, Winnipeg, Manitoba

Published with the assistance of the Ontario Heritage Foundation, Ontario Ministry of Culture and Communications.

Cover Photo (inset) Heintzman Piano Company factory, Toronto, c.1905.

Additional documentation, comments or piano-related questions are welcomed by the author, Wayne Kelly. He may be reached in writing by using the publisher's address.

Canadian Cataloguing in Publication Data
Kelly, Wayne, 1947–
    Downright upright: a history of the Canadian piano industry

Includes bibliographical references and index.
ISBN 0-920474-60-8

1. Piano makers – Canada – History.   I. Title

ML663.K45 1991   338.4'77862   C91-094845-3

CONTENTS

Introduction   7

Chapter One   Echoes and Epitaphs   12

Chapter Two   Early Canadian Keyboard Instruments   17

Chapter Three   Development of the Upright Piano   22

Chapter Four   "The Largest ... The Biggest ... The Best"   30

Chapter Five   Player Pianos, Piano Players, Reproducers, and Nickelodeons   36

Chapter Six   The Major Players, The Dominant Chords   42

Chapter Seven   The Pianos of Canada: A to Z   97

Chapter Eight   How Old Is My Piano?   126

Chapter Nine   Buyer's Guide   129

Chapter Ten   The Organ Makers   131

Chapter Eleven   The Final Chord   136

Giants of the Keyboard   139

Notes   148

Bibliography   151

Visuals Credits   153

Acknowledgments   155

Appreciations   156

Index   157

Mendelssohn's Wedding March

Felix Mendelssohn

With the Compliments of

The Mendelssohn Piano Co.
110 Adelaide St. West,
TORONTO.

Price 50 Cts

Introduction

Over the piano was printed a notice: Please do not shoot the pianist. He is doing his best.
– Oscar Wilde, Personal Impressions of America, 1883

The reality was worse than my nightmares. From a lineup of forty-two budding rural prodigies, my lot had fallen to the number two position.

It was June 1954. Mrs Margaret Joiner's semi-annual piano recital was a social highlight anticipated by countless thousands – or at least by the mothers of the anxious, hand-wringing waifs who were awkwardly settling themselves on the wooden slat chairs in the Appin Town Hall.

Forty-two. Hmmmm! Times two? Times five? That's 420 sweaty little digits that would paw the old Heintzman keyboard within an hour and a half. How I wished that time were past and I was home safe in my bed. I had never felt so sick. Mom called it nerves or something. Should I go to the washroom again? I need another drink of water. Is everyone looking in my direction?

Hours seemed to pass while the first melodious act echoed painfully around the room. Betty and Barbara Carruthers made the Dotty Dimple Waltz duet last forever. I closed my eyes and leaned on my mother's arm. The scent of her perfume made me think of lilacs. We had lilacs at our home – lots of them. Duncan MacFie and I were going to build a clubhouse in those bushes that summer. Duncan was my best friend. He didn't take piano lessons.

"WAYNE KELLY!"

I swallowed hard. My eyes welled up as I stumbled reluctantly toward the stage. "If only a tornado would strike," I thought. "A flash flood. Anything! I hope I don't wet myself."

Two hours later I sank into my bed. It was all over but the memory. But every six months for the next few years the dreaded recital had to be faced again. I wonder how many thousands of other young Canadian piano students have suffered through these events with the same fear and anxiety I experienced as a seven-year-old. Likely most of them.

Yet the thought of playing the piano was wonderful. When we got our first television in 1953 I remember moving hands and fingers along the arm of our old burgundy couch in imitation of those amazing pianists who regularly appeared

RECITAL
By Pupils of Margaret E. Joiner
Monday, June 28th, 1954 - at 8.30 p.m.
Appin Town Hall

Duet—Dotty Dimple Waltz.....................
................Betty and Barbara Carruthers
Circus Parade..........................Wayne Kelly
Uncle Joe Plays a CakeWalk Tune..Vickie Blackmore
Spring Song
Dancing Gayly........................Patsy Gillies
Skating.........................Rose Anne Gallagher
Duet—Little Ruby...........Irene and Barbara Graff
Petal Drift....................Barbara Carruthers
The Juggler
All Through the Night............John Thornicroft
Up the Hill..........................Mary Carroll
Dance......Elizabeth Foster and Penny Eichenberger
Beautiful Dreamer.....................Ronald Pole
Woodland Waltz....................Marian Murray
Purple Pansies..................Mary Ann McLellan
Trip to the Moon..................Beth McDonald
On Skates........................Judith Fletcher
Clarinet Solo...................Ingram McCallum
Spanish Dance.......................Ann Johnson
By a Garden Gate....................Sue Johnson
Nodding Daisies.................Barbara Graff
Beautiful Evening Star...............Irene Graff
Sailor's Race.......................Ronny Pierce
Swing in the Orchard............Betty Carruthers
Trio—Marche Brilliante....................
.........Sharon, Dorothy and Mary Carroll
Doll's Dream......................Dianne Johnson
Country Gardens..................Ronald Schiedel
Fairy Wedding...............Mary Lou McTaggart
Merry Sprite....................Elizabeth Foster
Sleigh Ride......................Bernice McDonald
Banjo Tune........................Judy Wayling
Hopak...........................Velma McLellan
In the Evening Shadows.............Lynda Gates
Reading ....Sheila Gates
On the Meadow....................Dorothy Carroll
Moonlight on the Lake.............Margie Jeffery
The Irishman Dances............Margaret Schiedel
Sonatina...........................Ruth Schiedel
Mocking Bird March.........Mary Ellen Gallagher
Dance......Elizabeth Foster and Penny Eichenberger
Three Blind Mice....................Kathie Joiner
Flower Song........................John McDonald
Magic...........................Ingram McCallum
Scherzino.......................Jo-Anne Edwards
Glow Worm.....................Sharon Carroll
German Dance..................Norma Thornicroft
In a Monastery Garden.........Margaret Galbraith
Sous Bois........................Catharine McNeil

Lunch will be served in the United Church basement

---

as contestants on the Wishing Well Ginger Ale Talent Show or some other such program. To be able to play as they did! What a thrilling prospect!

Appreciating such dreams, and imagining that their children must certainly possess secret talents, my parents somehow scraped the coins together over those years to give my three sisters and me the "necessary" piano lessons. My father's itchy foot and an ever-changing job with Canadian National Railways meant that we moved often. Two years here, ten months there, and it was on to the next town. But the piano teachers were always the same. They must be the same in most every town in the country. Weighty, perfumed women with little hankies stuffed in their cleavage and European names such as Madame Sharpzenflatz. Women who would always give you a pat on the head and usher you into plush dark rooms that smelled of geraniums. Geraniums and dust.

I didn't hate the piano, just the torturous lessons. I'm sure that those old piano teachers were genuinely interested in all their students and really wanted to see them make progress. But once you were past the Dotty Dimple Waltz stuff it was the foregone conclusion that all young pianists must spend the next eight or ten years wading through the mandatory Royal Conservatory of Music program. If only I had appreciated the importance of that dry old music. Likely I would be an accomplished – or at least competent – pianist today. But like scores of others who were coerced, bribed, or beaten into taking piano lessons, I just wanted to be able to play the "neat" songs, not all that Bach, Beethoven, and Brahms.

As is true of so many other Canadians, music was a very strong part of my early years. The inevitable radio, records, or TV were always serenading our home with song. My father sang constantly. My mother whistled. And it was generally swing. The swing music of Goodman, Dorsey, and Miller that they had courted to – and been courted with – during the mid-1940s. And after all, I had been named after one of those big band clones: Wayne King, "The Waltz King."

But the sounds issuing out of our old upright piano, more than from any other source, were the ones that filled our family home like air. Almost every evening in commanding ritual, my father rifled through a mountain of sheet music, selected six or eight "golden oldies" from the 1942 hit parade, and let his lean fingers glide along the eighty-eight until it was well past my bedtime.

Piano tuners and other musicians were regular guests in our home. Trading pianos the way many men traded cars, my father regularly introduced us to the "better" instrument.

"Listen to that tone! Just feel that action!" was the constant plea, as if he were trying to do a sales job on the rest of his household. He didn't have to.

By the time I reached Grade Six, we had fortunately settled in one town and would move no more. Mitchell, Ontario, was a town filled with music – in the schools, the churches, the clubs and halls, the streets. Music caromed through that little town like the balls in a busy pool hall on Saturday. When Dad and I later joined the brass band at the local Royal Canadian Legion, exciting musical horizons stretched my way. Secretly scrounging a key to the instrument room, almost every day after high school I spent time alone in the second storey of the legion kissing trombones and trumpets and sousaphones and any other brass I could wrap my arms around. I was in love.

After a half hour or so of puffing and panting, a further half-mile dash would bring me to Gordon Duncan's shop.

Gordon Duncan was a piano tuner. But he was more than that. He was a musician, a mechanical genius, an artist, a poet, a confidant. The run from the legion band room to Gordon's place not only put me within sight of my home – and the prospect of being on time for supper – but usually gave me the opportunity to spend close to an hour in the presence of a dozen pianos and a mentor to whom I have always remained grateful.

Regulating a player piano, striking correctly a Caribbean marimba, restringing a cello, or shaving a 1/1,000 of an inch off a saxophone reed – those were the golden calisthenics Gordon Duncan put me through every day. And on Saturdays, for the price of a six-pack of bottled chocolate milk and a dozen honey-glazed donuts, two or three other fifteen-year-olds were recruited to help Gordon move pianos. On end through dining-room windows, up rickety outside wooden staircases, on the back of farm wagons or old Ford pickups, down darkened hallways and across countless hardwood dance floors, we moved seventy-year-old upright pianos to every corner of Perth County.

I miss those days. My exposure to such a broad variety of musicians, instruments, and teachers was an invaluable experience – and one that has shaped my life. Many songs, fads, and music styles have come and gone. With a "jack-of-all, master-of-none" attitude I have turned fickle hand and mouth to many instruments. But after all the noise has faded, after all the other instruments have had their play, the piano calls me back like the lure of a siren. I still wish I could play better than I do. And performing for others is still not a great joy. But that said, the piano in my dining-room is an object I cherish for its theraputic value at the end of a long day.

Obviously, I am not alone. Millions of Canadians have had love affairs with the piano, and a multitude of talented people have cut their musical teeth on an old upright. At one time or another almost every household in the country had a piano. More common than today's VCRs, microwaves, or dishwashers, the parlour piano was a principal household appliance. Few are the adults who do not have at least some intimate piano memory in their background.

That the piano had once been an integral part of Canadian social life is manifest by lingering "piano" phrases still heard today. We speak of using someone as a "sounding-board" for our ideas, or having to "soft pedal" through a difficult situation. Janis McGill – the first girl I ever kissed – insisted that most boys wouldn't even look at her because she was one of those poor unfortunates who had "piano legs." Many Victorian homes in central Canada had a "piano window" in the main parlour. Generally a small rectangle, oval, or octagon of stained and/or bevelled glass, such windows were five to six feet from floor level, beneath which one would position the "required" upright piano. Writers of some post-second World War detective novels occassionally threw in a strangulation murder by means of a "pianowire necktie." There are still a few "watering holes" in this country where you can have a drink and be entertained at a "piano bar." And how many Grade Four music students still pose the joke: "What do you get when you drop a piano down a mine shaft? A Flat Minor!"

There are other examples, too. During the late nineteenth century, a cockney worker's chamber-pot was referred to as the "little piano."[1] From 1912 onward, the British expression "play the piano" meant to have one's finger prints taken.[2] By the 1920s the Anglo-Irish "piana [sic] that plays a pretty tune" substituted for cash register.[3] In Afro-American slang a single section of broiled spare-ribs was called a "piano."[4] And the expression "horse piano" was used across America to refer to a steam calliope.[5]

From the "dog-dirty," piano-playing, villain/hero of Robert Service's epic *The Shooting of Dan McGrew*, to Humphrey Bogart's intoxicated command "Play it again, Sam," to the sequinned, black and white, keyboard-design costumes of Elton John, piano motifs have figured strongly in our social consciousness and continue to exert influence in the lives – and vocabularies – of even those who may never have touched the instrument.

Canada was a major world producer of pianos. With hundreds of manufacturers having come and gone, surviving instruments are still found in every corner of the earth. The piano industry was a truly amazing one, and it made a wonderful contribution to countless Canadian lives.

This book is by no means the definitive record of the Canadian piano industry. While efforts have been made to list all known manufacturers and all brand-name pianos made in Canada, no doubt some have been overlooked. By detailing the stories of a few, many have been neglected. Yet, what follows, it is hoped, will highlight some of the outstanding people who have wandered across this stage of Canadian history and whose creativity, talents, and love of music have sounded a chord that still lingers in the hearts of those who treasure the piano.

As with many unreported aspects of the Canadian piano industry, few photographs of pianos were taken or survive. During the early 1940s mountains of old documents, records, and ledgers were consumed in "paper drives" that fueled the national war effort. Since the industry seemed to be in its death throes anyway, few individuals had the foresight to retain anything for posterity. The quality of the graphic materials presented herein is therefore less than optimum. Photocopies from scratched microfilm, third-generation photographs from faded pictures, advertising layouts from yellowed newsprint: these are the rule rather than the exception. In most cases, however, much care has been taken – in the darkroom and at the art board – to clean up the only available material without which a dimension of this account would remain in deep shadow.

The rise and fall of our piano industry testifies to the tireless efforts of an army of devoted, innovative Canadians – men and women who merged brilliant craftsmanship and marketing skill with the inward need most of us have to create our own "art." Eventually, the voice of this once proud industry was subtly supplanted by other voices: the phonograph, the radio, "offshore" piano imports. In its day, however, the upright piano had been a dominant symbol of Canada's Victorian era, a classic emblem of slower days, simpler times. As current world events move at laser speed awakening us to the fragile nature of our world, it is refreshing to pause momentarily and inhale the idyllic past. Canadians have loved – and still love – their old pianos. ♪

CHAPTER ONE

Echoes and Epitaphs

*His eyes went rubbering round
the room, and he
seemed in kind of a daze,
Till at last that old piano fell in
the way of
his wandering gaze.
The rag-time kid was having a
drink; there was
no one else on the stool,
So the stranger stumbles across
the room, and
flops down there like a fool.
In a buckskin shirt that was glazed with dirt
he sat, and I saw him sway;
Then he clutched the keys with his talon hands
– my God! but that man could play!*
– Robert Service, The Shooting of Dan McGrew, 1907

On Saturday, 9 January 1988, after months of negotiations with federal and provincial ministries, the Ontario Development Corporation, and assorted financial institutions, the assets of the last piano manufacturer in Canada fell to the auctioneer's gavel. At a large, two-storey yellow-brick factory in Clinton, Ontario, several thousand people had gathered: the quiet and nostalgic because they remembered what used to be; the sad and tearful because they and their fathers and their fathers' fathers had worked there; the hungry and eager because they hoped to bid on the carcass of one of the hundreds of partially assembled instruments.

The Sherlock-Manning Piano Company Ltd., successor to the W. Doherty Company which had started in Clinton back in 1875, had weathered many financial storms before, having witnessed more than a dozen different principals and owners over a 112-year period. The cruel rap of the auction hammer sounded the close of an era.

Several days earlier, a visitor to the company's premises would have seen walls with large windows, staggering galleries of sunlight and shadow on once-active workbenches, row upon row of hardwood trestle-tables waiting anxiously for the return of craftsmen who had laid down tools and gone for lunch. But the one o'clock whistle did not blow. The workers did not return.

For more than a century, tens of thousands of finely crafted organs, player, grand and upright pianos, and, in more recent times, a dozen different models of apartment-size pianos had left these doors and been shipped all across Canada and to every corner of the earth. In 1913 Doherty instruments were found in the United States, South America, Europe, India, and every part of the British Empire. Even the Czar of Russia had one.[1] Not long after Sherlock-Manning bought the Doherty operation in 1920, and added several new piano models, the company was one of the largest piano exporters in Canada. (See Figure 3.)

But the Sherlock-Manning Piano Company had not been alone. In the past 175 years, close to 220 individual organ and piano manufacturers have come and gone in Canada. With 95 per cent of these operations located in south-central Ontario and the Montreal area, several thousand Canadians have worked at this trade in the industrial heartland of our country. And in many cases small towns of two or three thousand people have played host to a company that for years was the major employer.

The social impact of the piano in Canada cannot be overstated. Evolving from a status symbol in the 1880s to an almost mandatory household appliance by 1910, the piano was the hearth around which generations warmed in song. As *The Economic and Industrial History of the City of London, 1855–1930* put it, "Amusement and entertainment still centred very largely in the home. Music was a great attraction for young and old alike. Those who could neither play nor sing could enjoy listening. A group of young people in the home brightened the evening with song and

Figure 3. Beneath a forty-foot banner, a CNR freight train is poised to pull away from the Sherlock-Manning piano factory, Clinton, Ontario, 1925. Owner Frank Sherlock can be seen at the engine cab door. This load was destined for British Columbia, Australia, New Zealand and the Orient.

instrument. If friends dropped in to spend the evening, music always had its place in the entertainment provided."

The piano was the first and only form of creative expression most households would know. Many hours each week were spent in the presence of the keys. (What a contrast with today's fragmented family sitting silently around a somewhat cold and impersonal VCR.) "Mailorder" brides moving to the Canadian west often insisted that log cabins and sod huts be equipped with a piano. In schools, lodges, church basements, community halls, and public buildings in every corner of every province, the piano was a piece of standard equipment.

The piano was considered so important to the Canadian household that a newspaper editor was moved to write in 1916:

Music in the modern home has come to be a requisite of the first importance to the cultured and refined, the magnet which attracts the son and daughter to the fireside of the parents and the charm which makes home a haven to the tired mind and body after the day's toil and commercial strife. Musicless homes, according to the results of investigation, are in the majority of circumstances those forgotten by the son and daughter after a few years in the business world. The modern inventions which have been brought into action to instill a spirit of repose and refinement in the residence – the electric light, telephone, well modelled furniture – these have played their part in the uplifting of citizenship to its present lofty plane. Yet there is one influence which has done more perhaps than any of the rest in instilling the refining influences – the organ or piano. [2]

Thousands of this country's most talented

Figure 4. "Living room and dining room of a typical working-class home, circa 1920," from the Hines Photographic Collection, London, Ontario. The piano is described as a Mason & Risch.

> # Terms of Payment.
>
> Pianos under $150—$10.00 cash and $4.00 per month, without interest.
> Pianos over $150—$15.00 cash and $6.00 per month, without interest.
> Pianos over $250—$15.00 cash and $7.00 per month, without interest.
>
> If monthly payments are not convenient, please state what method you prefer—quarterly, half-yearly, or at certain fixed dates. We wish to know what terms will suit you.

Figure 5. Gourlay, Winter &Leeming ad from the Globe, 1904.

musicians have had their earliest musical interests piqued on the black and white keys of the parlour piano. And as the instrument became accessible to almost every Canadian family, it is not surprising that this product was one of the very first consumer items to be sold on terms. (See Figure 5.)

By the mid-1850s a number of pianos had arrived in Victoria and Vancouver by way of Cape Horn. And while "musical and social evenings" occasionally brightened the lives of the locals, it was the Fraser valley gold rush of 1858 that created a demand for the instrument in the new Canadian west.[3] Many years later, with the beginning of the Klondike goldrush, dozens of instruments were ordered by saloon owners and travelling musical groups. Arriving in Vancouver by train, crated pianos were hoisted into the salty holds of ferrys bound for Skagway, Alaska. One enterprising troupe, the Sunny Samson Sisters Sextette – Essie, Tessie, Bessie, Ethel, Maude, and Nellie – "pursuaded strong man Mike Mahoney to carry their piano to the top of the Chilkoot Pass on their way to Dawson, where they intended to entertain miners, who showed their appreciation with gold. Mahoney made a special harness to get the piano on his back for the 1,200-foot climb. The tragedy in this feat of strength is that the North West Mounted Police at the summit of the pass refused to let the sisters into Canadian territory and they had to go back to Skagway, a town reported to be 'lousy with pianos' at the time."[4]

Most piano companies saw the early advantage of putting salesmen on the road. Orders rushed in. A Heintzman piano was baggage on the first transcontinental train – destined for the Klondyke. By fishing boat, that same company landed the first grand piano on Prince Edward Island. And a northern Manitoba mining community received the first ever aircargo piano.[5]

In 1907 the small Ontario town of Uxbridge had a piano company that was in financial trouble. Flamboyant salesman Hillary McGuire swung through the "River City" circuit from Halifax to Montreal and in just twenty-eight days persuaded 125 households that an Uxbridge piano would save their children from lives of sin and degradation.[6] About 1910, Heintzman salesman Bill Fletcher toured Ontario backroads with an upright on a horse-drawn wagon. In winking collusion with the wagon driver, he would seek out the most prosperous farms in a township, pretend to lose a wheel close by, and then insist that the farmer help move the precious instrument into his home, safe from the elements. Bill would then commence a coy recital of Brahms, Bach, and Joplin. It was a rare event that the piano had to be loaded on the miraculously repaired wagon.

Frank Sherlock had been a traveller and salesman in the years 1911–13. He reportedly crossed the country dozens of times by train, peddling the latest Doherty (later Sherlock-Manning) wares. Orders came in by the hundreds. The Canadian piano industry was booming.

Many of the larger Ontario manufacturers set up showrooms and retail shops in major cities in western Canada, thus contributing to the fact that very few piano factories were established there. (See Figure 6.) Additionally, with ever-improving rail-freight service, a boxcar of pianos shipped from Toronto could arrive in Vancouver in as little as two weeks. Mail-order pianos were popular too. The T. Eaton Company regularly offered two or three upright styles at the turn of the century and included in its catalogue elaborate half-page ads for pianos. These could be shipped to rail points anywhere in the Dominion.

There were many reasons for the rise of the Canadian piano industry. The most important was the unsatisfactory nature of imported European pianos. Because of the size and fragility of the piano, it often concluded a long Atlantic voyage in less than perfect condition. Further, since the cold, dry Canadian climate made many instruments warp, shrink, and become virtually untunable, even the best European pianos soon were not worth the price of their passage.

The other reasons involved economic change. As Canada industrialized, the increase in inventions and labour-saving devices gave rise to more leisure time. Also, the growing economic sophistication of central Canada created a demand for entertainment while also increasing the amount of money available for consumer spending. The importance of both these points is emphasized by Craig. H. Roell in *The Piano in America, 1890–1940*. "The rise of the piano industry," says Roell, "highlights the transition of [North American] society from one dominated by the work ethic of the nineteenth century to one devoted to consumer culture in the twentieth. As industry and society mechanized and electrified, workers in the twentieth century laboured for fewer hours per week. Work and sacrifice became less valued in a culture that increasingly honored leisure, recreation and consumption." [7]

Figure 6. The retail rooms of the Doherty Piano Company, 324 Donald St., Winnipeg, c. 1907.

CHAPTER TWO

Early Canadian Keyboard Instruments

The indefatigable pursuit of an unattainable perfection, even though it consist in nothing more than in the pounding of an old piano, is what alone gives a meaning to our life on this unavailing star.
– Logan Pearsall Smith, Afterthoughts, 1931

The oldest musical instruments in this country are the percussive shakers and rattles that accompanied ancient aboriginal ceremony. To this musical heritage European immigrants in the late sixteenth and early seventeenth centuries added woodwinds, lutes, viols, and guitars. Champlain's "Order of Good Cheer" (c. 1608) was perhaps the first European ensemble put together in Canada for the white man's enjoyment. The earliest reference to a keyboard instrument is found in a Quebec City Jesuit journal that documents the arrival of a French organ in February 1661 with a second organ following in 1663. [1]

More than 100 years pass before Canadian music history records any further references to keyboard instruments apart from mentions of early clerical use. But in 1776 one Friedrich Glackemeyer, an apparently capable, professional German musician, arrived in Quebec and in the winter of 1783 began offering music instruction to a local family. Until then two female pupils had been relegated to "a miserable old spinet which they had bought at Three Rivers, there being only one piano in all Quebec." [2]

Glackemeyer quickly created a base of music students and a desire for ownership of instruments. By 1788 he proudly advertised that he was able to fulfill such desires and supply several musical items to the population. His ad in the Quebec Gazette read: "Two new excellent Piano Fortes with a neat leather cover warranted to be of best tone and to stand in tune a long time ... the best Harpsichord, Piano Forte and Guitar strings ... Tuneing hammers and Pitch Forks." [3]

By June 1789 the first Canadian music school was established in Montreal. And in a newspaper notice in September of that year, patrons of the arts were advised: "Mr. Mechtler begs leave to inform the Ladies and Gentlemen of Montreal that he has settled himself in this city as a MUSIC MASTER, and intends to teach the

FORTE PIANO, HARPSICHORD and VIOLIN: he therefore flatters himself that he will meet with encouragement from those Ladies and Gentlemen who may please employ him." [4]

While a growing number of teachers began offering private music instruction throughout Quebec and Ontario, it was the slow appearance of regulated teaching standards that drew ever-increasing interest in keyboard artistry. Historian Timothy McGee states that "music instruction in the public school system began with the appointment of James P. Clarke to the Toronto Normal School in 1847. Halifax put music into the school curriculum in 1867, and by the end of the century schools in many of the larger cities offered music classes."[5] The availability of quality instruction was therefore a main reason why Canada's mid-ninteenth century population could support a musical-instrument industry.

That music was becoming a sophisticated business in Canada during this period is further confirmed by McGee, who suggests that "an important indication of the growth of musical activity in Canada during the nineteenth century was the increasing number of people making a living in music. Aside from performers, this included vocal and instrumental teachers, as well as merchants selling instruments and books of music. Music publishing houses opened in Halifax, Saint John, Quebec City, Montreal, Toronto and Hamilton, and by Confederation they had published over six hundred works by Canadian and foreign composers." [6]

The earliest known pianoforte builder in Canada was a German craftsman, Friedrich Hund, who constructed several instruments in Quebec City in 1816. By 1827 the firm of Mead, Mott & Co. was active in Montreal and it maintained a lucrative business there until 1853. Nova Scotia, New Brunswick, and Ontario also witnessed the arrival of many talented European craftsmen who established small piano businesses from 1830– 1850. [7]

The imigration of numerous German piano craftsmen to North America had a dramatic influence on our fledgling industry. According to musicologist Alfred Dolge, writing in 1911, twenty-two contemporary American firms were of German origin. [8] And while no country-of-origin statistics are available for Canadian firms, the influence of German tradesmen was no doubt proportionate throughout the Canadian industry and is confirmed by the abundance of German names appearing in company records and patent files.

Musical instruments frequently made the arduous journey with the early white settlers of western Canada. As early as 1833 a piano pleased the soldiers at the Red River Academy, in what was to become Winnipeg, [9] and several more domestically produced square pianos had arrived

Figure 7. Ad from the Globe *(Toronto) 9 November 1847.*

there by the mid-1840s. 10

In 1840 York Factory on Hudson Bay saw the arrival of a piano by York boat – a type of heavy freight canoe. Chief Factor James Hargrave had purchased the German instrument in London for £36, demanding that it be "seasoned for any extremity of climate." 11

One of Canada's foremost music historians, Helmut Kallmann, documents the appearance of keyboard instruments in Winnipeg by quoting the 1888 report of a correspondent of the *Music Journal*:

> *On his arrival here in 1882 your correspondent found only one miserable little melodeon and two pianos in the whole place. In 1883 our Methodist friends advanced a step and invested in a very fair reed organ, the English Church people shortly after following suit. The same year witnessed a large increase in the town, not only of musical instruments, but of talent. In 1884 the Presbyterians, following the good example of the other churches, purchased a good reed organ. The town could then boast of seven organs and eight pianos. Towards the end of this year we organized the "Birtle Musical and Dramatic Club." From then till the spring of 1887 things went smoothly, new organs and fresh talent appearing every month or two. Early in the spring of 1887 the Presbyterians substituted a small but good "pipe organ" for the reed organ they had hitherto used. They now claim to have the only pipe organ in the country west of Winnipeg."* 12

Kallmann also reports that while a violin, clarinet, or concertina added only little weight to a pioneer's baggage, it was a problem of a different sort to transport pianos around Cape Horn or on carts across the prairie plains and rivers and over mountain passes ... yet this was done. The men detailed to York boats, Red River carts and Victoria-bound barques knew pianos as the most cumbersome, contrary and delicate devices civilization had thrust upon them. Pianos were packed on mules at a rate of a dollar a pound from Quesnel to Barkerville, the centre of the Cariboo gold region.

Notwithstanding the forbidding costs and difficulties of transporation, pianos were essential amenities in this atmosphere. As James McCook put it, "On the prairies pianos and pemican had a priority." Part of the money received from [the] first 'bumper crops' of 'Manitoba Hard' [wheat] went for upright pianos. The vogue for pianos was due largely to the pioneer women, for many prospective brides from England and eastern Canada made it a condition that they be provided

Figure 8. Ad from the London Free Press, *9 January 1857.*

with a piano in their homes. Women associated these instruments with the dignity and conventionality of the older communites they had left." 13

According to the *Encyclopedia of Music in Canada*, "The 1851 census lists 4 individual piano builders or companies in Toronto, 10 in Montreal and 3 in Quebec City. By the year of Confederation (1867) larger piano manufacturing firms were being established." (Prior to the mid-1860s, however, almost all piano companies consisted of a single craftsman, who, with perhaps one assistant, produced one or two instruments a month.) The same encyclopedia lists 130 different piano manufacturers and/or brand names that have appeared in Canada since 1860. (But with a further 110 or so companies and name brands having been discovered, a total of more than 240 firms and/or "name" pianos will be considered in this book.)

Musical interests in Canada have historically mirrored immigration patterns. From the early seventeenth to the mid-eighteenth century, French folk songs and a small amount of clerical music were dominant. But following the British victory on the Plains of Abraham in 1759, and the subsequent arrival of United Empire Loyalists from the Thirteen Colonies, chamber music, band

Figure 9. A typical Canadian melodeon, c. 1865. Known by some manufacturers as a harmonium, this small, compact reed organ was nothing more than a mouth organ with a keyboard. Generally unequipped with "stops" (which alter the sound by allowing air movement across preset combinations of reeds), the melodeon was popularized in Ontario, Quebec, and Atlantic Canada from 1850–75. Two pedals, pumped alternately, moved push rods that operated a horizontal bellows, which in turn allowed forced air through the reed/key stop mechanism. (38" x 20" x 31" high; manufacturer unknown)

Figure 10. Ad from the Ottawa Daily Free Press, 28 October 1882.

concerts, song recitals, and opera performances gained speedy popularity. [14]

As author Clifford Ford suggests in the introduction to *Canada's Music: A Historical Survey*:

> *"It must be kept in mind that the social makeup of the immigrant groups had a decisive effect on the type of musical performances ... The greatest bulk of the immigrants [1600–1760] belonged to the rural lower class, where folk music naturally would abound, whereas a sizeable number of immigrants [1760–1900] later came from the middle class, from which amateur music-making, musical craftsmanship and music teaching were derived."* [15]

Since 1875 the principal piano constructed in Canada has been the upright (cottage or cabinet) grand. And while some horizontal grands – from baby to concert size – as well as many "square" pianos (until the 1880s) have been made, it is the upright piano that is most deserving of our attention. ♪

Figure 11. A popular square piano sold in Canada about 1870.

CHAPTER THREE

Development of the Upright Piano

*Mater artium necessitas
(Necessity is the mother of invention)*
– old Latin saying

I don't think necessity is the mother of invention. Invention, in my opinion, arises directly from idleness, possibly also from laziness. To save oneself trouble.
– Agatha Christie, An Autobiography, 1977

T he history of the pianoforte as it developed in Germany, Italy, France, Great Britain, and the United States has been well documented in dozens of scholarly works. The long horizontal grand pianos that flourished in eighteenth-century drawing-rooms were true works of art, characterized not only by their ornate cabinetry and design but by their ever-improved actions and tonal quality.

The early vertical or upright pianos were simply grands turned on end with action modifications. As early as 1735 Christian Ernst Friederici had designed one in Austria, and several survive in European museums.[1] England's William Stodart developed an upright in 1795, and his example was followed by John Broadwood & Sons Company of London in the years before 1815. (See Figure 12.) According to musicologists of the time, these pieces were generally of poor quality and dangerously top heavy.

With the dawn of the nineteenth century the square piano began to grow in popularity. A more compact instrument than existing grands, the square was the obvious choice for many Europeans living in cramped urban quarters. As the century passed, the square style itself gave way in Europe to the cottage, or upright, design. It remained in vogue in North America well into the 1880s, but met its end in 1903 when American piano manufacturers meeting in Atlantic City voted to terminate "this disgusting instrument" in favour of the upright. At a cost of more than a hundred thousand dollars, several trainloads of square pianos had been gathered from manufacturers and dealers across America. A pyramid fifty feet high was erected on a vacant lot. With solemn anticipation – then feverish cries – the attending crowd witnessed the kerosene dowsed heap become a gigantic piano pyre.[2]

The first North American upright piano

Figure 12. Upright grand piano built by John Broadwood & Sons London, England, c. 1815.

built by John Isaac Hawkins, an English engineer living in Philadelphia, had received patent protection in 1801. The piano was less imposing than the hulking European styles, because Hawkins utilized the waste space from keyboard to floor for a design of diagonal strings over a compact steel frame. (See Figure 13.) With an overall height of just fifty-four inches, and requiring scarcely ten square feet of floor space, this new invention appeared to be a fine alternative for the would-be piano owner. But as A.J. Hipkins, author of the 1896 publication *Description and History of the Pianoforte*, explains, "It was a remarkable bundle of inventions but not a musical instrument." Due to the unsatisfactory tone, the Hawkins upright was generally not accepted and production ceased.

While some of the old European master craftsmen sneered and chuckled at the folly of such things, innovative young thinkers continued to experiment with overstrung and diagonal string configurations that would eventually result in an instrument that was not only space-efficient but musically acceptable.

With his first upright piano design of 1811, England's Robert Wornum developed a system of diagonally running strings and a corresponding action of outstanding precision and response. Apart from more recent ideas concerning damper placement, Wornum's design ideals for upright piano actions have remained basically unchallenged. [3]

German uprights came into production by 1835 and rapidly attained a reputation for excellent durability and tone. As exports increased, particularly from the 1860s onward, German pianos were imitated by North American manufacturers. Many copyright and patent scandals ensued as the "old world" craftsmen battled colonial ingenuity. In 1852, German immigrant J. Maas produced his own type of upright in Berlin (Kitchener), Ontario.[4] And an 1858 report concerning Knott & Sons in Hamilton described that city's first cottage (upright) piano, stating: "The very shape of a cottage is something strange in this country, where the less elegant and more cumbersome square is the prevalent form. The Canadian woods have been found admirably suited for the making of the instrument. From the pine sounding-board to the black walnut case, all the wood Mr. Knott uses is of Canadian growth, and it really gives us confidence in the vastness of our resources when we find this to be possible." [5]

In 1866 a patented device that was a "combination piano, couch, closet and bureau with toilet articles" made a brief ripple through the trade of the day. "The stool housed a workbox, a writing desk, a looking glass and a set of drawers." And who would poke fun at such an invention? After all, the 1854 Daniel Hewitt design "whereby the strings were attached to the wall of the house to save the expense of the piano frame" had met relative success in Britain. 6

A point made earlier concerning the horrendous effects of the Canadian climate on nineteenth-century pianos cannot be overemphasized. The piano, an instrument of some 6,000 pieces, most of them wooden, is extremely vulnerable to changes in humidity. The early European imports to Canada were made with woods not well seasoned to withstand our dry winters. Placing them in parlours that were primarily heated with a wood or coal stove further added to the trauma of winter dryness. When spring arrived and windows were opened wide, the humity levels from the damp days of April and May settled in piano woods. After several years of such shifting extremes, many instruments were good for little more than firewood.

Canadian piano manufacturers spent many decades and experimented with a remarkable number of inventive designs in attempting to remedy this problem. But perhaps more than anything else, the realization that piano woods had to be kiln dried properly was the most important discovery that allowed the industry to produce just the right piano for the Canadian climate. By the 1890s William Doherty and his talented employees at a Clinton, Ontario, factory had learned the secret. Working with a maze of underground tunnel kilns on his property, Doherty developed a method of wood treatment that was later adopted by most Canadian piano makers.

Former Sherlock-Manning employees Murray Draper, his brother, and father spent a combined total of 156 years with early Doherty methods of piano construction. Concerning the wood-drying systems, Murray recounts:

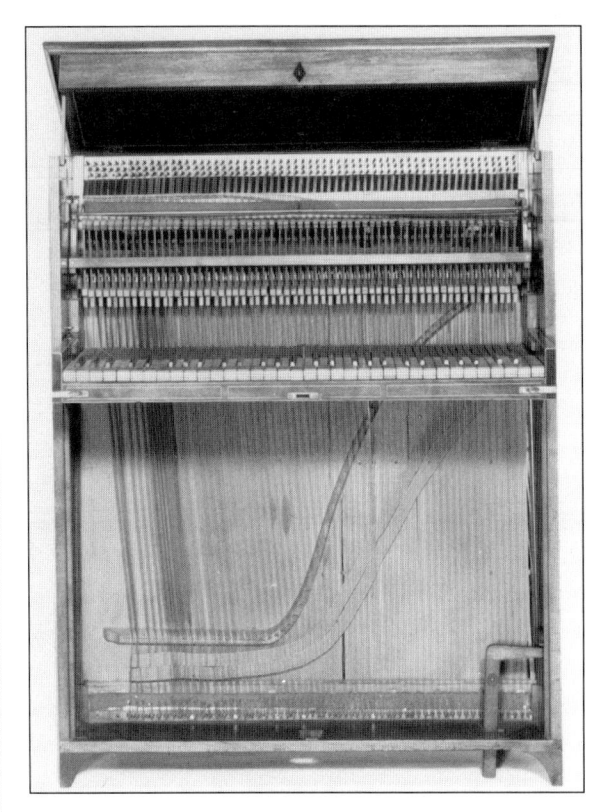

Figure 13. One of the first upright pianos in America, made in Philadelphia by John Isaac Hawlins in 1801.

> *In connection with drying, live steam was piped to the kilns as a heat source. Also, used exhaust steam from the engines (still hot) would be forced through the underground tunnels for extra heat and moisture. To dry lumber, heat was used to reduce the moisture content of the wood, which could hold from 40 to 60 percent moisture. But steam must be circulated through the boards to keep the outsides from drying out first. Ideally, a lot of steam is used the first couple of days; then, each day more heat and less steam are used so gradually the heat gets to the centre and then (the board) dries from in to out. Drying was a very important part of the system. If it was hurried to save a day or two, the results could be that later on the lumber would crack or warp and really never remain stable."* 7

Such discoveries and ingenuity helped create pianos that not only endured in this country but have been popular in every climate on earth.

Our vast timber stands in British Columbia have added immeasurably to the Canadian industry. The sounding-board – the most critical component of the piano relating to its tone – was found best constructed from western spruce. But not just any old spruce tree would do. The enduring favourite, thin sheets of solid Sitka spruce, have come from the north side of trees growing on the north side of mountains. The extra cold and lack of sunlight on such tree sides mean little branch growth, and so a clear wood free from knots and uniform in grain was available. Many piano companies in the past (and even the Yamaha Music Company of Japan today) have purchased timber rights for such stands of BC spruce.

Creative thinking and mechanical brilliance have been a hallmark of the Canadian piano industry throughout its history. While numerous British and American patents had been granted to Canadian manufacturers prior to Confederation, the first piano patent (#242) was filed under the country's new patent legislation on 29 December

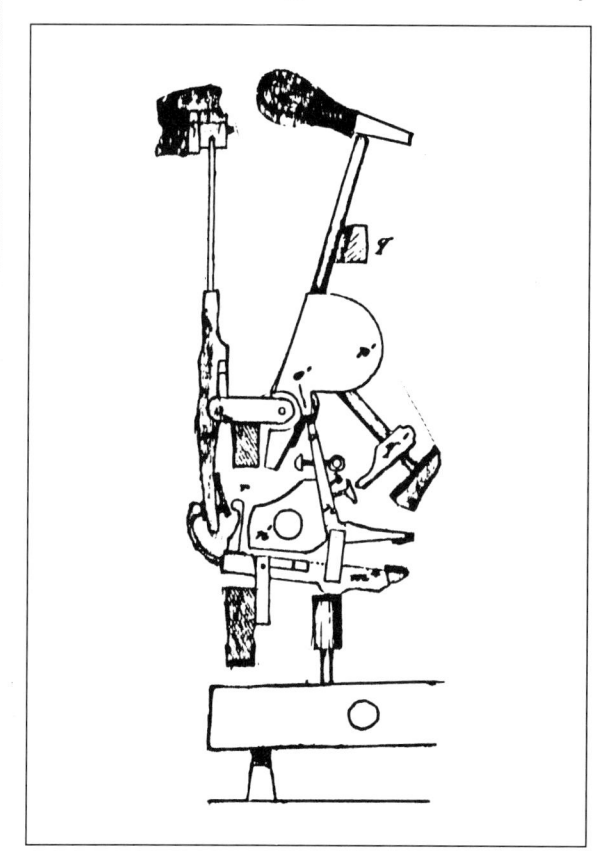

Figure 14. The first piano-related patent filed under Canadian patent legislation of 1869. Patent #242, it was filed by inventors Joseph Gould and Freedom Hill, Montreal, 29 December 1869.

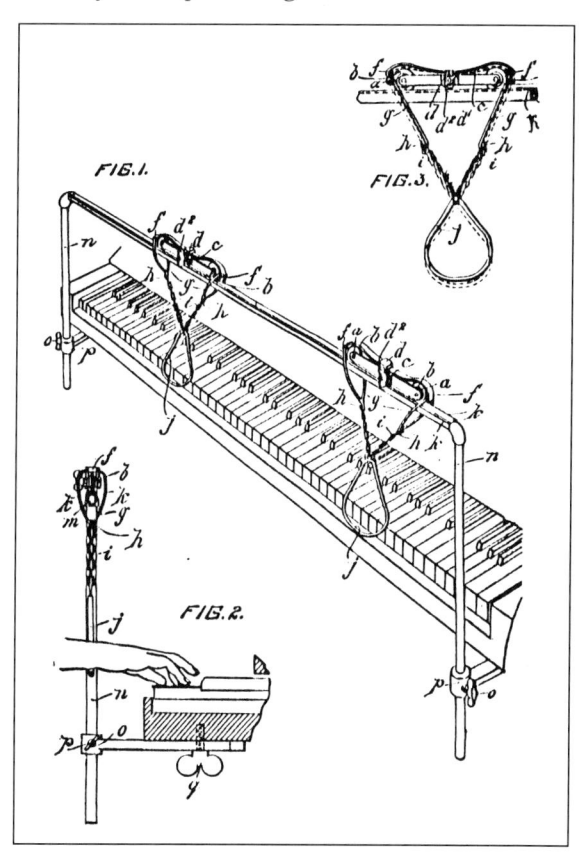

Figure 15. "Hand Guide For Pianos" – patent (#73478) filed by William Bohrer, Montreal, 22 October 1901. The claim described a rod assembly with two moveable carriages that was to be attached directly to the piano. For anyone who has had their hands rapped by a piano teacher for letting their wrists droop while playing, the purpose of this strange invention will seem humorously significant.

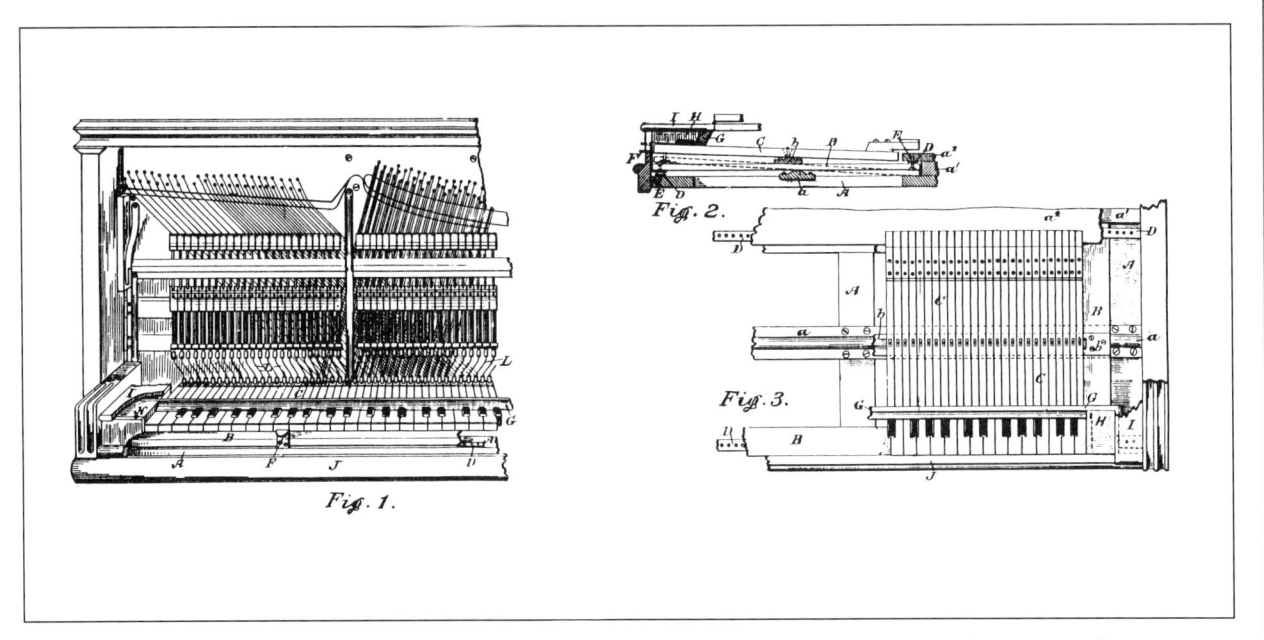

Figure 16. "Marcy's Transposing Piano Action and Key Board" invented by Alexander Marcy, Clinton, Ontario, 24 september 1891. (Patent #37459) An interesting system whereby the push rod (abstract or sticker) between the end of the key (capstan) and the action bottom (jack) was an offset metal shaft (see "L" in "Fig. 1"). The claim described these "connecting lifters" as able to deflect the action up to half an octave to the left or right. Marcy, a native of Montreal, arrived in Clinton about 1888. He no doubt worked at the Doherty piano factory, although no surviving records indicate that this piano was produced by that firm.

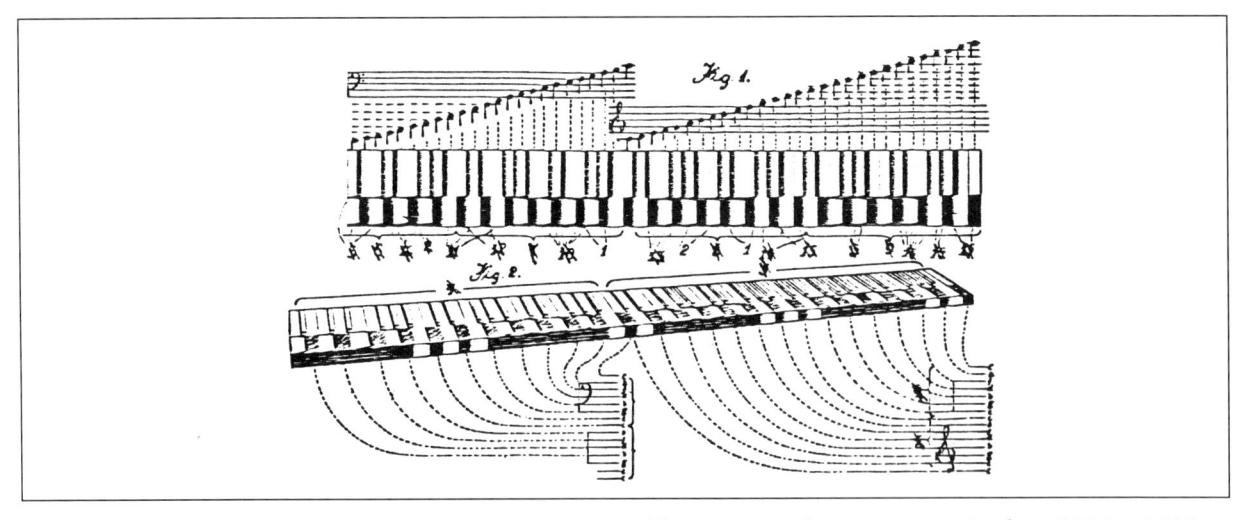

Figure 17. "Keyboard For Musical Instruments" Invented by A.M. Smith, Westmount, Quebec, 16 May 1911 (Patent #133,175). The patent claim details a method of colour coding certain keys so as to help a pianist distinguish "natural notes written on the lines of the music staff, the other marks to correspond to the natural notes written in the spaces." It is not known whether such a system ever came to fruition.

1869. Since then scores of inventions have been registered to the piano makers of Canada. (See Figure 14.)

From systems of coloured keys and mouse-proof cabinets to elaborate transposing devices and the ever-elusive "better" piano action, the industry has witnessed innovations ad infinitum over the years. Jealously guarded secrets and the constant rush to put the "new and improved" instrument on the market did, however, create an air of distrust between business competitors. As Matthew Willis (late of the Montreal piano firm Willis & Company) put it, "Piano people have always been a suspicious lot!"

That observation was not unusual. Many piano tuners, technicians and other tradesmen have made similar comments. The piano industry at the turn of the century could be likened to the highly competitive computer industry today where security systems, protective measures, suspicion, and jealousy also reign supreme.

The Canadian Patent Office has files that document many early piano ideas complete with intricate drawings and occasionally photographs. A selection of six such registered patents follows, with several others appearing later in conjuction with piano companies.

So much more could be said about the bril-

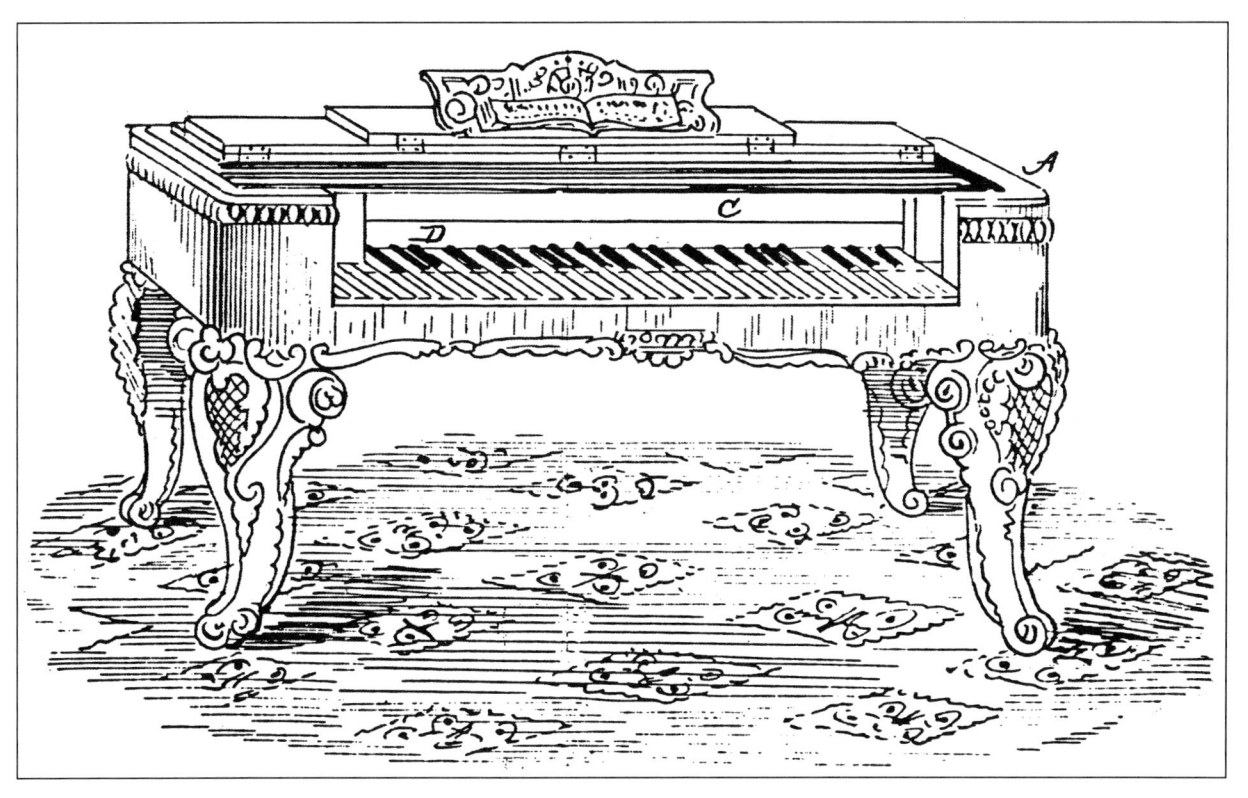

Figure 18. "Improvement on Pianos." Patent filed 8 January 1883 by Dennis McCarthy and George R. Davis, Saint John, New Brunswick (Patent #16,082). The claim describes "a fingerboard faced or partly faced with mirror glass whereby the instrument is prevented from being scratched and the instrument improved in appearance." This is a fine example of the "Square" piano style. Inherent design and action faults meant that these instruments went out of tune and suffered regular mechanical frictions largely because of changes in temperature and humidity. By 1890 few square pianos were being manufactured in Canada.

liant technical changes regarding frames, mechanical actions, keyboards, hammers, damper systems, and sound-boards. Truly, the piano with its thousands of parts – like the automobile – is a marvel of human inventiveness.

By the early 1840s budding inventors Abraham and Samuel Nordheimer had opened a piano dealership in Kingston. Their years of experience in handling European and American imports would eventually move them to produce their own fine-quality instruments. Thomas Mason, Vincent Risch, Octavius Newcombe, Alexander Willis, William Doherty, Louis Pratte, George Heintzman, Dennis Karn, Frank Sherlock, Wilbur Manning, Damase Lesage, and many other talented inventors would likewise enter the trade before the close of the nineteenth century. Their individual stories will highlight their achievments. ♪

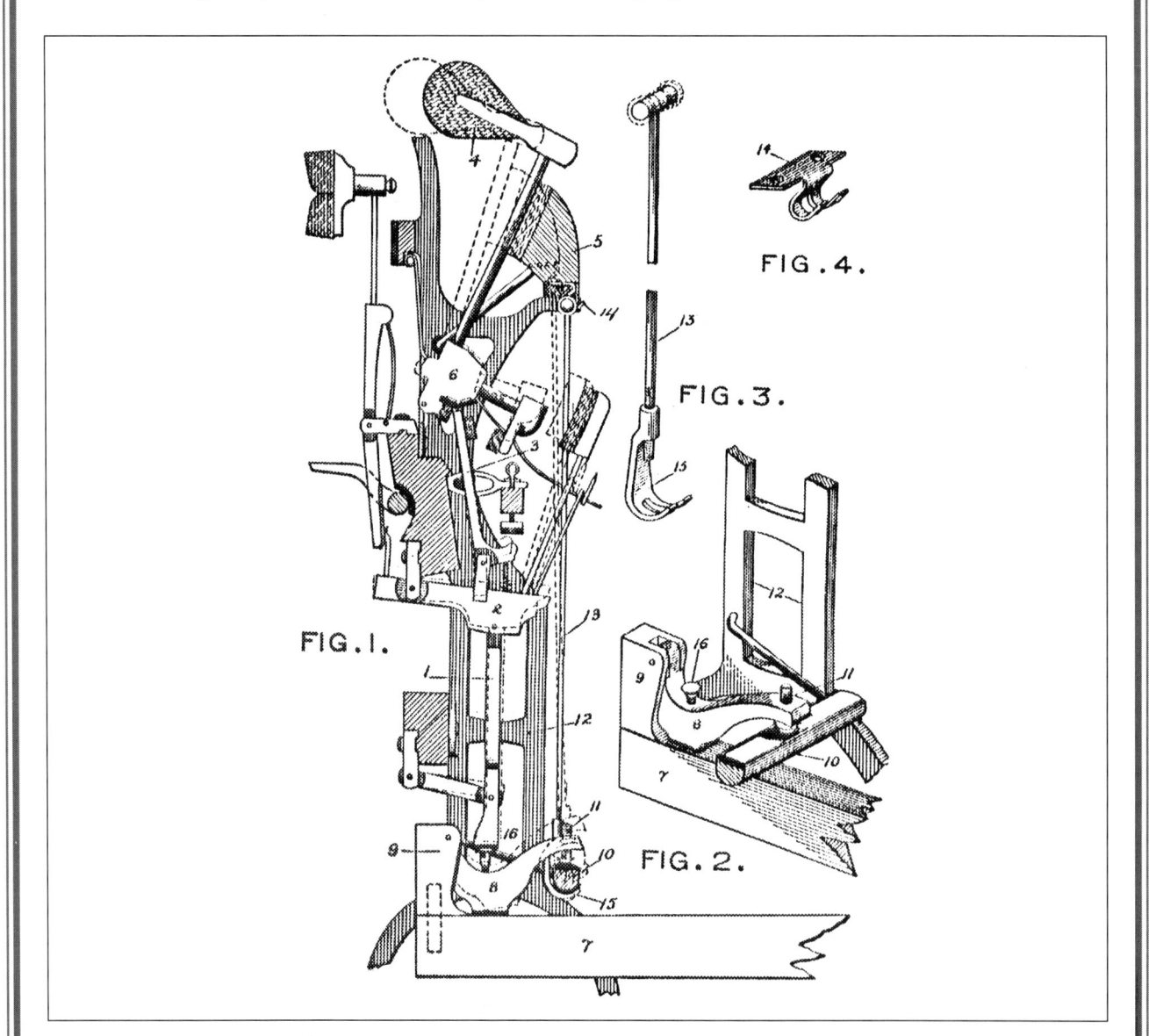

Figure 19. "Piano Action (Patent #93,498) – Otta Glatt and William J. Richardson, Toronto, 6 February 1905.

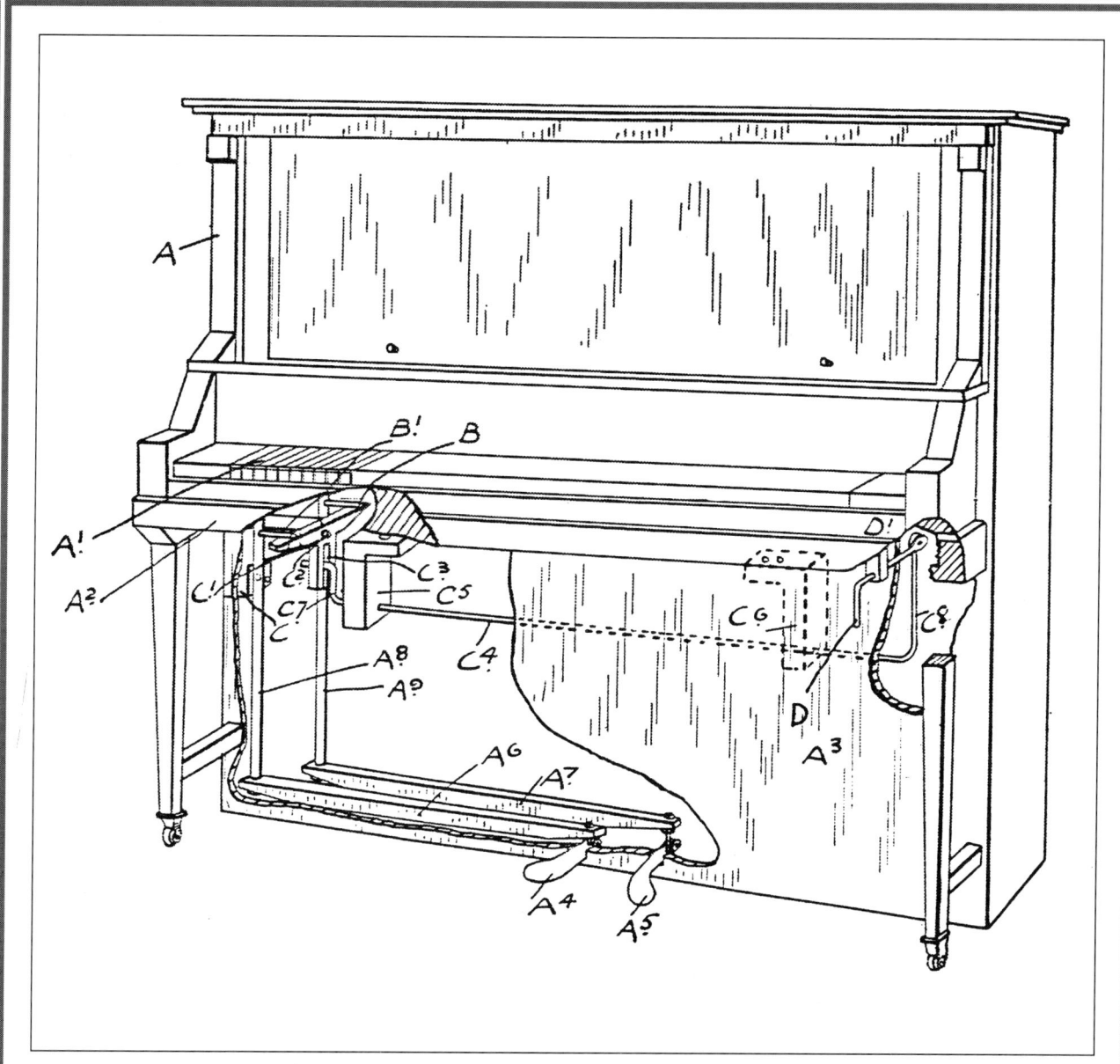

Figure 20. "Pedal Mechanism for Pianos." Invented by Ralph Colwell Brand, Peterborough, Ontario, 9 February 1909 (Patent #116,562). This is just one of hundreds of North American patents for piano pedals. Many companies used this as a selling feature, indicating a special technique or tone that could be achieved from the use of their particular pedal design.

CHAPTER FOUR

"The Largest ... The Biggest ... The Best"

The codfish lays ten thousand eggs,
The homely hen lays one.
The codfish never cackles
To tell you what she's done.
And so we scorn the codfish,
While the humble hen we prize,
Which only goes to show you
That it pays to advertise.
– Anonymous

About 1870, American Joseph P. Hale had begun marketing pianos with entrepreneurial style. A self-made man who had accumulated a small fortune in the crockery trade, Hale bought a large interest in an eastern piano company and started a system of production-line manufacture and merchandising hitherto unknown to the North American piano industry.

Called the "father of the commercial piano," Hale is also notable for having started the "stencil system." According to a 1911 publication, Hale "would stencil his pianos with any name desired by the buyer, which law permitted. Thus the dealer, especially the big jobbers from the American West, commenced to sell some pianos with their own names on the fallboard, or even cast into or screwed on the iron plate."[1] In this way the piano surreptitiously became the first substantial consumer item to bear meaningful brand names.

In the early days of stencilling, abuses and deception were rife. A good example concerns the world-famous Steinway & Sons Company formed in New York in 1853. Look-alike pianos bearing names such as "Steinvey," "Steinwebb," "Steinmann & Son," or "Steinmetz" are instances of misspellings deliberately used to create names that looked similar to that of the well-known brand.

Many companies also used assorted trade names or "stencils" apart from their own firm name so as to allow for distribution in certain geographic areas; or a stencil name would be applied to a fallboard for a line of pianos sold by a department store. In Canada the T. Eaton Company is an example of a department store that sold – but did not manufacture – their own "name" brand of pianos.

Often the names of composers appeared as the stencil name on certain lines of pianos manufactured by large companies. The "Beethoven" piano was made by Shaw in Montreal. Mason & Risch had a "Schubert" and a "Chopin," while

Lesage made a "Schumann." Toronto's Stanley Pianos turned out the "Liszt" and the "Mozart Symphony" was a name used in Canada by Newcombe. Even today, offshore piano companies still produce stencil-name pianos designed for the North American market. Yamaha distributes the "Steigerman" while the "Morganstein" is made by the Fuji Piano Company.

And even before pianos fell victim to the stencil system, entrepreneurs such as William Doherty distributed a choice of seventy-four organs using an assortment of names from his Clinton, Ontario, plant.

By 1905 at least five Ontario companies presented advertising claims that their factory size, sales records, export trade, quality products, or some other such attribute made them "Number One." Bell boasted being "the largest maker of pianos in Canada"; so did Karn in Woodstock and Dominion in Bowmanville. Whaley-Royce said that its product was "unexcelled in tone, faultless in construction." Gourlay pianos were "not merely first class, they are something better." And Morris, with its "most modern and finest equipped piano factory in Canada," claimed that it had "the highest grade pianos" possible.

Figure 21. Trade cards c. 1905.

With ad agencies practically nonexistent at the turn of the century, the responsibility to "push" the company product generally fell to one of the bright people in the office. Catchy slogans and logos, cartoons, and clever newspaper artwork were the "make or break" factor for many piano companies. Giveaways such as calendars or printed yardsticks were a popular way of keeping a piano name in front of potential customers, whether they were checking the next phase of the moon or administering the rod of discipline to the kids. But two sales gimmicks stand out as almost universal in the Canadian industry.

The trade card was the first to appear – about 1895. A small, highly coloured lithograph ranging in size from a standard postcard down to debutante dance-card proportions, the trade card was the most popular handout. Stacks of company cards with idyllic scenes of children or spaniels or lilacs graced the counters of many music stores and stationery shops of the day. On the reverse side waxy testimonials from dukes and dowagers spreading the merits of ownership were designed to woo even the most sceptical. Much originality accompanied this short-lived advertising blitz, but perhaps no trade cards were as poetic and artful as those of the D.W. Karn Company. (See Figure 21.) A dozen such cards have been found, many borrowing from nursery rhymes or popular phrases of the period turned to a mawkish bent.

A second outstanding handout was the company song, given to each purchaser or prospective purchaser. Reams of sheet music rolled off the early presses. None of these appear to have become enduring classics and might best be described as "silly little ditties." "The Dominion Waltz," "The Ennis March," "The Silver Bell Two-Step," or the "Whaley-Royce Two Step" were just some of the catchy titles. The Metropolitan Toronto Reference Library has an impressive collection in its sheet music files of some forty songs composed for fifteen Ontario piano companies. (See Figure 22.)

A further means of calling attention to the merits of a company's product was to reproduce, in decal form, replicas of medals and awards received at trade shows. Virtually every piano manufacturer in Canada entered European and American trade-fair competitions. And with legions of categories in which to qualify, it was not unusual for almost every firm to walk away with at least one medal. Stencilled around the company logo as if they were priceless Roman coins, such citations were commonly displayed as an indicator of the apparent excellence of the product. (See Figure 23 and 24.)

Several efforts have been made to estimate the number of pianos produced in Canada in the years before the First World War. One set of figures, which several Canadian musicologists have quoted, states that 12,000 pianos were made in Canada in the year 1900, with annual production reaching 30,000 instruments in 1912. But there may be reason to question the accuracy of those numbers.

While there were a few government departments requesting production figures at the turn of the century, there simply were no travelling "watchdogs" or bureaucratic auditors to check actual production quantities. As long-time industry man Matt Willis asserts, "You could write down any figure you wanted. I knew of one company [in the 1940s] who reported production figures as 3,000 for one year." He adds sardonically, "If they turned out 300 pianos that would have been a closer number. I know. I was in their factory every couple of weeks."

It is tempting to view a long-gone industry through rose-coloured glasses so that it appears filled with honesty, camaraderie, and cooperation. To do so, however, is to distort the hard realities of the past. The fact is that some piano companies, eager to capture public admiration and future sales, were not beyond padding the numbers. Persuading a rival that your production was higher than theirs was well within the methods of

Figure 22. The front cover of the sheet music for "The Bell Two-Step," written for Bell Pianos Ltd., Guelph, by Charles J. Orth, c. 1908.

Figure 23. The fallboard from a Karn piano illustrating the award decals and branch offices.

*Figure 24. A stencil on the iron-frame plate of a 1906 Heintzman piano.
The awards include two from Australia won in 1877.*

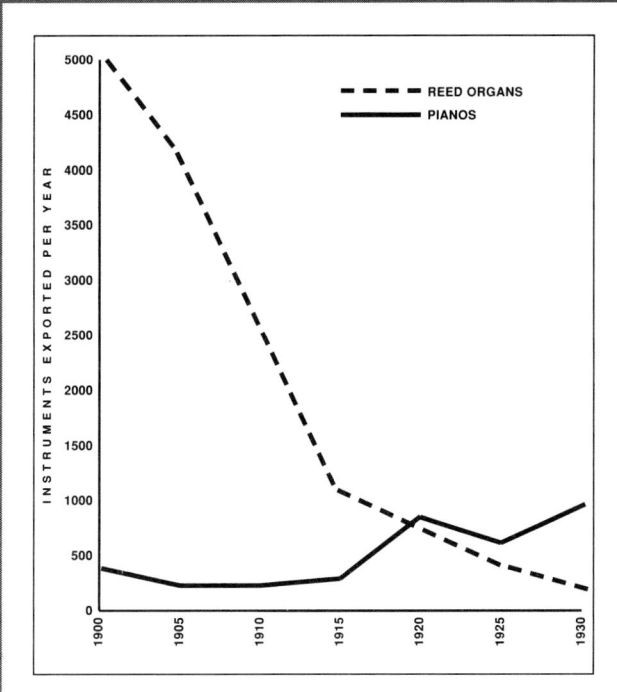

*Figure 25. Canadian Organ and Piano exports 1900-1930. Source: **The Canada Yearbook**, vol. 1900-30, published by the Dominion Bureau of Statistics.*

many organizations which competed fiercely for piano sales.

Export figures, which were documented by Canada Customs, may be fairly accurate. But all too often, for the reasons noted, data collectors may have been hoodwinked about total domestic production. This was no doubt especially the case during the difficult, scramble-to-survive times when the piano was in decline.

Drama – love affairs, arson and disastrous fires, union turmoil, power struggles between corporate rivals, patent scandals, fortunes made, fortunes lost – has always swirled around the piano industry. The remarkable stories that regularly unfolded through the history of this Canadian business were the stuff of Hollywood movies, as will be seen shortly. ♪

CHAPTER FIVE

Player Pianos, Piano Players, Reproducers and Nickelodeons

Picture the pleasure you would derive from your piano if you could have a great virtuoso become a guest in your home to entertain and to educate! The musical value of this instrument cannot be overestimated, as it places the piano on the highest level of perfection, making better piano music than ever before possible. Comparatively few people are familiar with the wonder of this new instrument. It is conceded to be the ultimate musical accomplishment, and homes of culture that cherish the finer things of life desire its possession.
– 1921 Sherlock-Manning brochure for the "Reproducing Piano"

Since mechanical human beings have applied labour-saving inventiveness to almost every aspect of their lives, it was just a matter of time until the precious piano fell victim to automated action. As early as 1890 a mechanical piano player called the "Vorsetzer" or "push up" was patented in Germany. This unit was "pushed up" to the piano keyboard where a housing containing sixty or more mechanical fingers would then begin striking the keys from above, cued by the perforations on a rotating paper roll that would be set in motion by a foot-pedal and treadle arrangement.[1]

This invention came to be known as the piano player (not to be confused with the player piano) and was a separate appliance – generally on wheels – that the user could roll up against any brand or style of piano. (See Figures 26 and 27.)

One of the earliest Canadian piano players was manufactured in 1901 by Werlich Bros. in Preston, Ontario. Not being a piano manufacturer per se, the Werlich company was dependent upon the piano industry for the sale of its product. Less expensive American imports (made by the famous Wurlitzer and Seeburg companies) soon put the Preston firm and the few other Canadian manufacturers out of the piano-player business.

The piano player survived only four or five years. As was the case with the large high-fidelity and early stereo consoles of the late 1950s – those coffins on legs – the cumbersome piano player was soon viewed as a household redundancy. The invention that sounded its death-knell was the player piano. Why have two large cabinets in the parlour when one would suffice? The 1906 Mason & Risch ad included here explained the benefits of the complete system. (Interestingly, both their piano player of 1904 and their new player piano of 1906 were called the "Pianola.") (See Figure 28.)

Almost every major piano manufacturer in Canada offered a player piano during the 1906–1925 period. With only a few manufacturing their own player components, the majority simply installed mechanisms supplied by companies such as Toronto's Otto Higel. The Higel device allowed virtually any upright to be converted to a player piano, and even a few horizontal grands were modified with player actions. (The Willis Piano Company of Montreal produced several player grands.) The Higel company, which grew to be one of the country's largest suppliers of piano keys, actions, wires, and assorted components, also became one of the major suppliers of player-piano rolls in Canada. (See Figure 29.)

As each year progressed more refinement came to the player piano. Nordheimer featured the "Human Touch" expression control and stated in its 1912 literature that "the addition of this wonderful invention to the present efficiency of the Nordheimer Player places it on a plane by itself, and makes the Nordheimer the most Perfect Player made in Canada." [2]

During the First World War, Robert J. Flaherty (later known as an outstanding filmmaker and producer of "Nanook of the North") spent much time in the Northwest Territories in search of iron-ore deposits. Among his most valued pieces of equipment was a player piano. When the fall pack-ice forced Flaherty to abandon his small boat, he moved his equipment – including the item the Inuit called "the singing box" – to safe quarters on the Belcher Islands on Hudson Bay. Author James McCook recounts that "when Flaherty left in the summer he presented the piano to an Eskimo named Wetallock. Winter came again and Wetallock tried to get the piano

Figure 26. Each year for several decades the "Nordheimer Piano Music Book" was published. The book contained a dozen or so popular and light classical tunes, each headed by an engraving depicting a certain product or aspect of Nordheimer's downtown Toronto retail store. This 1904 publication illustrates "The Piano Player Department." The Chases & Baker Piano Player was made in Buffalo.

into his igloo, without success. He put it on a sled and took it 85 miles over dangerous sea ice to Great Whale River on the mainland of Quebec. There he found that Flaherty had gone to Fort George, 186 miles south. Without hesitation Wetallock guided his dogs down the shore and arrived at Fort George in the middle of the night to present the astonished man with his piano."

In 1920 Sherlock-Manning added a transposing device to its popular player piano. With the mechanical shifting of the roll to the right or left side of the "tracker bar," the device operated by a lever "will change the song to the desired key and is as easy as applying the foot pedal." That same year, Sherlock-Manning's "Style 120" featured the "Instantaneous Self Acting Accenting Bellows" and a "Bass and Treble Dynamic Control," two systems that were operated by levers. The company claimed that reproduction from a paper roll could now be "as sensitive as possible with accent of the solo or melody notes as desired, permitting the most delicate and expressive tone shadings."

Further refinements to player pianos included the "Reproducing Piano," which boasted unmatched reproduction quality from a special patent roll. The addition of a silent motor to drive the system also enabled the listener to "assume the position in which he can best enjoy the music." 3

Apart from Mason & Risch, Nordheimer, Sherlock-Manning and Willis, player-piano manufacturers in Canada included the Bell, Doherty, Dominion, Evans, Heintzman, Martin-Orme, Morris, Sumner & Brebner and R.S. Williams companies.

The logical extension of the electric reproducing piano was the nickelodeon. A forerunner of the jukebox, the nickelodeon found a home in restaurants, ice-cream parlours, pool halls, and saloons from coast to coast. 4 With yards of pneumatic tubing, electric sensors, and vacuum switches, the nickelodeon was an incredible invention. Snare and bass drums, tamborines, whistles, xylophones, banjo, and other sounds all accompanied the regular piano play induced by a coin-operated device (hence nickelodeon) that played special paper rolls. (See Figure 31.)

A note regarding company names.

Figure 27. Ad for Mason & Risch piano player from the Globe, 6 July 1904.

In the following sections it may be noted that certain inconsistencies exist concerning the proper names of various piano manufacturers. This occurs for the following reason.

The official legal name of most firms changed relative to their principle product. Thus we find the Bell Organ and Piano Company Ltd. (c. 1880–95) when their major commodity was the reed organ. Later, as the piano gained prominence we find Bell Piano and Organ Company Ltd. (c. 1905–25) as the official name. The Doherty operation in Clinton, Ontario, is a classic example of repeated name changes, having held no less than six distinctly different corporate names in the period 1875–1920. Therefore the accounts that follow respect the existing legal names that certain firms may have employed at various times. Generally the surrounding text material and dates will allow the reader to approximate the period in which official corporate designations may have occured. (Precise dates for corporate name changes were not researched.) Additionally, while the abbreviation "Ltd." may have been included with the corporate name of most companies, appearing on literature and logos, it will generally not appear in most company accounts. ♪

Figure 28. Ad for the Mason & Risch "Pianola" player piano from the Globe, 3 October 1906.

Figure 29. A player piano roll as distributed by the Otto Higel Company, Toronto, in 1919.

Figure 30. A prospective buyer tries a 1909 player piano at the Sherlock-Manning liquidation auction, 9 January 1988.

Figure 31. A partially restored nickelodeon built into a 1921 Sherlock-Manning player piano.

CHAPTER SIX

The Major Players, The Dominant Chords

BELL PIANO AND ORGAN COMPANY LIMITED

What is a home like
Without a Bell organ?
A prison, asylum; a jail
Where no one will stay but a culprit
Unable to find any bail.
– from "A Panegyric on the Bell Organ" by George Norrish, Guelph poet and long-time Bell employee [1]

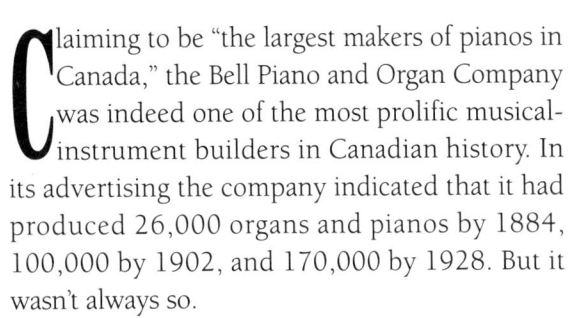

Claiming to be "the largest makers of pianos in Canada," the Bell Piano and Organ Company was indeed one of the most prolific musical-instrument builders in Canadian history. In its advertising the company indicated that it had produced 26,000 organs and pianos by 1884, 100,000 by 1902, and 170,000 by 1928. But it wasn't always so.

The business began in 1864 when brothers Robert and William Bell, under the company name of Bell Brothers Melodeon and Organ Manufactory, started turning out one melodeon a week from a small, upper-storey frame building on Wyndham Street in Guelph, Ontario. Within just three years they could not keep up with the local demand for their fine-quality instrument which the press of the day described as "a four legged black beetle with polished back and sides." [2] (See Figure 32.)

With a guiding motto that "every piece must be the best" and an early business credo that demanded constant expansion, the firm grew faster than any other industry in the city. Building after building was erected or taken over until in 1895 almost an entire city block between Woolich and Wyndham streets was occupied by the company. (See Figure 33.) By then it was known as W. Bell & Company, William having long ago emerged as the dominant figure in the operation.

Accompanying this rapid physical growth was the reputation Bell instruments began acquiring. In 1889 music director Edward Fisher complimented the company on the quality of the piano it had supplied to the Toronto Conservatory of Music. "The tone is remarkably pure and brilliant throughout," Fisher wrote, "while the bass is deep and powerful. The mechanism is apparently perfect, the touch elastic, and in appearance the entire piano is a work of art." [3] With a troupe of salesmen covering the globe by the early 1890s,

Bell organs and pianos soon graced the regal chambers of Queen Victoria, and other monarchs as well as the homes of the wealthy and prominent in every part of the world. An 1895 business profile of William Bell and his world-famous instruments noted that "one of his products has been acquired by the Sultan of Turkey, who doubtless finds pleasure in its alluring tones after a hard day with the Armenian question. If 'music hath charms to soothe the savage breast,' then the Turk is to be congratulated upon his possession of a musical instrument made by hands that find their daily occupation in our fair city." 4

William Bell was a tireless worker. Apart from managing the affairs of his own company, between 1883 and 1897 he was president of the Globe Building and Loan Company, president of the Guelph Junction Railway Company, president of Traders Bank of Canada, and vice-president of Manufacturers Life Insurance Company. 5

About 1878 Bell's oldest son, William J., began learning his father's business, and at age seventeen he was sent to England for the purpose of establishing a branch of the company there. Staying in England for ten years, William Junior whipped up European sales from the London branch to the point where two-thirds of the Bell production in Guelph was funnelling through the British office.

The elder Bell remained actively involved with the firm until an accident forced his retirement in 1897, at age sixty-one. Meanwhile, young William emulated his father's expansionist philosophy. From the London offices – known distinctly as the Bell Piano and Organ Co. Ltd. – in 1889 he arranged to buy out his father's interest in W. Bell & Co. For several years afterwards, most corporate decisions were made from the offices in England. 6

The economic crisis of 1896–97, when management at the Guelph complex attempted to maintain profits by forcing a wage reduction of 8 per cent, was the signal for disgruntled Bell employees to address a number of unanswered labour grievances. By 1902 they had formed branch No. 34 of the American-controlled Piano and Organ Workers Union – the first union in a Canadian musical-instrument company. (See Figure 35.)

Like his father before him, William J. Bell had multitudinous interests in commercial and municipal affairs. By 1900 he had already accepted a position as vice-president of the Federal Life Assurance Company. And as a member of the Guelph Board of Trade, Bell proposed an experiment in municipal ownership of gas, light, power, and railway. His 1902 suggestion that Guelph become the first city in Canada to put its affairs entirely in the hands of municipal commissioners won him praise and press coverage from coast to coast. 7

Figure 32. Ad for the famous Bell "Diploma" melodeon as it appeared in the Guelph Mercury, 13 October 1870.

Figure 33. Bell factory #2, c. 1895. With a large lumber storage area across the street and a main line of the Grand Trunk Railway passing through its front yard, the company had an ideal location. Fire destroyed this building on 16 July 1975.

BELL PIANOS AND ORGANS

SUPERIOR IN
Tone, Quality,
Construction
and Finish.

Full description to be found in our Catalogues.
Mailed free on application to

THE BELL ORGAN and PIANO CO. (Ltd.)
Guelph, Ontario.

OVER 75,000 OF OUR INSTRUMENTS NOW IN USE.

5-1-y-om

Figure 34. Ad from the Farmer's Advocate and Home Magazine, 1 October 1895.

Figure 35. Bell employees formed the first Canadian branch of the Piano and Organ Workers Union.

Meanwhile, the fortunes of Bell Piano and Organ Co. Ltd. continued to improve at home and abroad. Its policy of advertising the merit of its instruments far and wide is evident from the scores of ads that appeared in newspapers of all sizes across the country. One series of ads, entitled "Little Bell Biographies," endeavoured to educate the masses concerning the lives of classical and contemporary piano masters. At the conclusion of dozens of these regular advertising installments, the entire collection was compiled in booklet form and offered free to anyone who requested it.

Labour turmoil seems to have subsided from 1907 or so onward as a result of company incentives, and the workers' own pride in producing one of the most sought-after pianos in Canada. The annual company picnic, where the bosses played with the boys, was a social event much anticipated by Bell employees. One such 1916 summer gathering on a farm near Bullfrog Pond, on Eramosa Road, was a roaring success. Ragtime piano ballads, baseball, and barrels of beer made locally by the East Kent Ale Company, made the occasion an outing to remember.

After 1920 business gradually declined as consumers wound up gramophones, cranked up Model Ts, and found other forms of entertainment that caused dramatically lower sales for piano companies all over the world. On 11 April 1928 the Bell Piano and Organ Company passed into the hands of a syndicate headed by John S. Dowling of Brantford, Ontario, who, despite valiant efforts, failed to revive it. The company declared bankruptcy in 1934. The assets were picked up by Lesage Piano Ltée. of Ste Thérèse-de-Blainville, Quebec, which continued using the Bell name for fifteen years.

Bell upright serial numbers
1895 – 5000	1897 – 7000	1899 – 8600
1900 – 9000	1903 – 12,000	1905 – 14,000
1907 – 18,000	1910 – 21,000	1912 – 24,000
1917 – 29,000	1918 – 30,000	1919 – 31,000
1923 – 33,000	1924 – 34,000	

W. DOHERTY & COMPANY*

In the year 1875 I commenced the manufacture of organs with a capital of $5,000 and employed one man. In 1876 I built a hand shop and employed eight men. We rented our power and machinery and did the case work in McCartney, Thompson and Scott's planing mill. All our organs were sold retail as they cost us more to manufacture than we could get for them from the trade. At the close of the year we found we had lost $2,000 on the year's business.
– William Doherty,
Clinton New Era, 19 January 1900

Sustaining a business loss of that amount in the 1870s would have forced most men to abandon the folly of trying to start an organ business in a town of 2,000 people. But as the account continues:

"We changed our system of doing business the next year. We now wholesaled our organs and retained our retail business as well. Our output increased and we thought we were making a little money, but after balancing our books, we found we had lost again, this time $2,300. Our capital was pretty well shattered. Nothing daunted and with the proverbial Canadian pluck, we tried again in 1878. We had at least acquired a knowledge of the requirements of the profession. We now decided to cease retailing and sell to the trade only, and for cash or on short time, to the best houses, for our banking facilities were at that time very meagre." 8

William Doherty, born on 21 March 1840 to Irish immigrant parents in Burford, Ontario, came

Figure 36. William Doherty, c. 1900. To everyone in Clinton, he was known as "W.D."

to Clinton in 1868. Establishing a furniture and music store, he had become a distributor for Bell organs by 1874. After he discovered the immense popularity of the organ among Huron County residents, Doherty decided that these instruments were not so complicated that he couldn't make them himself. His one-man, one-helper business of 1875 became an operation of one boss, and eight workers a year later. By 1879 a building on Raglan St was turning out 100 instruments a month, and the company had expanded to three manufacturing locations by 1897.

All this came to a screaming halt with a devastating fire on 1 February 1898. But drawing on his reservoir of "proverbial Canadian pluck," Doherty hired a contractor and Irish labourers and had a new factory standing by 14 May. An impressive tooling effort followed and on 10 August, just 191 days after the fire, his new East St factory shipped its first boxcar of organs, with a second following two days later.

---

* Most of the information for the Doherty (and later Sherlock-Manning) story comes from Murray Draper. The son of a craftsman who devoted fifty-six years to the trade, Murray himself spent fifty years with Sherlock-Manning. He is also the author of W.D. – The Story of Doherty & Sherlock-Manning (1986).

Always the practical businessman, Doherty taught his employees frugality. In later years his own frugal attitude was well demonstrated when faded, heavy canvas awnings from the office windows were used, along with tar, to patch portions of the factory roof. Doherty's determination to run a 'tight ship' was evident as well in the "Factory Rules" signs that were posted at strategic places throughout the plant. (See Figure 39.)

Doherty's business acumen dictated diversity. As early as 1900 the company catologue offered a choice of seventy-four organs using assorted actions and stops. And, in another vein, a barn and stable behind his factory witnessed an auction one afternoon in the fall of 1906 of "about sixty head of shorthorns, imported and grandly home-bred, being the entire herd of W. Doherty." 9

By 1900 the local economy was booming in Clinton, and Doherty had 180 employees on his payroll. Then two more fires, on 16 November 1901 and 15 February 1905, dealt serious setbacks to his business. In the case of the 1905 blaze, so much snow had fallen during the early morning that the 5:30 a.m. fire call went unanswered by Clinton's volunteer fire-fighters because they were unable to get the engine down to the factory. Fortunately the factory's own pumper was adequate for the job, and, with a favourable wind, damage was limited. 10

Figure 37. Illustration of the Doherty factory, c. 1910. The artist was very flattering. Portions of this complex were never built and there are three more rail sidings than ever existed.

The first pianos appear not to have been manufactured until 1905 or 1906, but within a few short years the firm, now known as Doherty Piano and Organ Co. Ltd., maintained large retail shops in Winnipeg and Calgary. During the heydays of the business, as much as three tons of coal a day were required to heat and power the Doherty complex. By 1913 grand pianos had been added to the long list of products turned out by the Clinton factory and the Doherty name appeared on instruments shipped to England, Scotland, Germany, the United States, New Zealand, Australia, India and Russia.

As an ongoing precaution against future fires, and possibly for insurance reasons, night watchmen were employed about 1907. Part of their nightly task was to make a round of the entire factory and "punch in" at a numbered key station, thus imprinting the time and location onto a paper dial locked within a time clock that each watchman carried in a leather pouch. This dial was then inspected by an office clerk the next morning so it could be verified that the physical inspections of the plant were actually taking place regularly during the night. As one can imagine, after many uneventful, long nights, a tardy watchman would rather put his feet up and snooze in the warmth of the boiler room than make the cold, lonely round through the darkness of the factory. As Murray Draper reports:

> "A favourite trick was to unscrew the boxes [key stations] on the first round and carry all the keys to the boiler room and then punch the clocks. However clever this was, it would soon be detected by the office, as it was hard to punch as regularly as the legal system. Just before I entered the business, this infraction had been detected and countermeasures had been taken. Because the constant night-by-night removing and replacing the boxes had worn the slots of the screws, new screws were put in. In due course they showed wear, so some genius removed the screws and drove in 4" spikes. As an added twist, he had previously hacksawed slots in the spike heads! Thus the feelings of the watchman can only be imagined as he struggled to turn out the spikes."

Doherty was well liked by his employees and staff turnover was low. Camaraderie and loyalty pervaded the company. One long-time employee, seventy-year-old Sammy, was known not only for his meticulous, consistent production habits but for his punctuality. One morning when he didn't show up, word soon buzzed around the plant that old Sammy had died. At someone's suggestion a collection was taken up and flowers were sent to the house. Shortly after lunch, Sammy arrived, thanked everyone for the flowers, and apologized for having slept in. Ironically, just two weeks later Sammy did die during his sleep.

In June 1910 George Yates, formerly a superintendent with Morris Piano Company, Listowel, was hired and immediately given oversight of the Doherty piano department. Within two years 1,500 pianos a year were being manu-

Figure 38. William Doherty's home on East Street was adjacent to the factory property. It was heated with steam from the boiler room and lit with electricity generated there.

FACTORY RULES

W. DOHERTY PIANO & ORGAN CO. LTD.

1. All employees are required at their places ready for work when the starting whistle blows.
2. Faithful service is required from all employees for the full working period without allowance for personal preparation prior to the blowing of the quitting whistle.
3. Care must be exercised in the use of the time clock. Workmen must not hurry, nor crowd or jam each other while registering their time.
4. Employees must give due notice and make satisfactory arrangements when a temporary absence is desired. Workmen who are detained by unforeseen or unavoidable conditions must promptly notify their foreman stating the probable duration of the absence.
5. Workmen are required to give undivided attention to their work. Wandering or loitering in other departments of the Factory will be under discipline of the department foreman, who is expected to promptly interfere to prevent undue waste of time by his own workmen or work men from other departments.
6. No work other than directed by the foreman, under the Superintendent's approval, will be permitted.
7. No smoking, lighted pipe, cigar or cigarette allowed throughout the main Factory buildings.
8. Boisterous and threatening language or assaulting a fellow employee during working hours or on the premises is strictly forbidden and will not be tolerated.
9. No intoxicating liquor allowed on the premises.
10. None but employees are allowed in the works during working hours. (Visitors with the Superintendent's consent are exempt from this rule.)
11. Employees are cautioned against wasting supplies or materials.
12. Violation of any of these rules will be subject to reprimand for the first offence: repetition will incur dismissal.
13. The foremen are depended upon to cooperate with the Superintendent to make these rules effective.

D.S. Cluff, General Manager.
1912.

Figure 39

Figure 40. The Doherty hockey team, 1912. In the back row, far right, with C.D. printed on his sweater, is Caryl Draper. This young man was destined to do more than just spend his next fifty-six years in the piano business. Draper was instrumental in the development of the first "apartment size" 43" high piano in 1924. At his right shoulder is one of William Doherty's sons.

factured. By 1915, company ads claimed that better than 70,000 Doherty instruments were in use "thoughout the civilized world."

Two former Doherty employees, J. Frank Sherlock and Wilbur N. Manning, had left the company in 1902 and started Sherlock-Manning Organ Co. in London. In 1920, three years after old "W.D." had retired, the pair bought the Doherty business. William Doherty died in 1924.

The Doherty story continued for another seven decades as part of the development of the Sherlock-Manning company.

Doherty upright serial numbers:
1905(6) – 1,000   1909 – 1,800   1910 – 2,000
1912 – 3,000   1915 – 7,000   1917 – 10,000
1920 – 16,000
(after Sherlock-Manning takeover of 1920)
1921 – 91,000   1924 – 95,000 1927 – 100,000
1930 – 102,000   1936 – 105,000

Contrary to references in piano atlases, the Doherty piano name did not remain in use after about 1937.

Figure 41. Doherty line pianos in a display at a trade show in Wellington, New Zealand, 1925. Sherlock and Manning had been in control of the business for five years by this time. The 43" high piano became extremely popular.

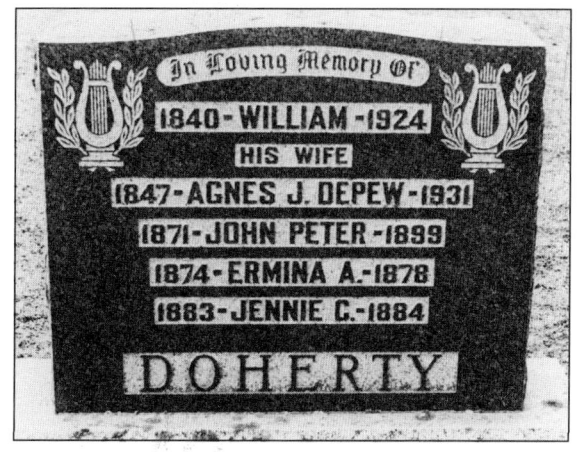

Figure 42. William Doherty's gravestone in Clinton cemetery. Fittingly, the lyres on each side speak volumes of the man who filled the lives of countless thousands with music.

DOMINION ORGAN & PIANO CO.

Two young men with a love of music and a good business sense put their heads together in 1870 and started a melodeon company. The instrument had already gained wide use in Ontario, largely because of the marketing work of the Bell Company. For A.M. Darley and William Robinson, the notion that they could make a living producing musical instruments – instead of toiling behind the plow – was a dream come true. Little did they know that their humble early efforts would produce one of the largest organ and piano manufacturers Canada would ever see.

Operating from a corner of the "Sons of Temperence" hall in Oshawa, Darley and Robinson took the name Oshawa Organ and Melodeon Mfg. Co. Within three years their growth demanded expansion to larger quarters. A new partner, Mr H. O'Hara, was admitted to the firm and the entire operation was moved five miles east to Bowmanville. By 1875 the name Dominion Organ Company had been coined.[11] A large, four-storey red-brick building was erected in the centre of town to house the organ complex and in 1879, when the decision was made to enter the piano market, expansion again became necessary.

In 1894 a major change in management would usher the company into an era of even

Figure 43. J.B. Mitchell (left) and J.W. Alexander on the office steps of the Dominion company, c. 1910.

greater activity. Under the direction of J.W. Alexander more buildings were added, the staff quadrupled to reach a total of close to 200 workers, and a huge export business was established.[12] By 1910 more than 80,000 instruments had been produced and branch outlets were to be found in Germany, England, Australia, New Zealand, South Africa, and Russia.[13]

The company's vice-president, J.B. Mitchell, is worthy of some mention. Not only was he the principal inventor at Dominion, and thought to be one of the most brilliant minds in the Canadian piano industry, but in 1916 he became mayor of Bowmanville. Mitchell promoted the town's largest industry far and wide. With a finger constantly on the fickle pulse of the buying public, Mitchell patented and introduced several lines of high-quality gramophones, something that helped the firm prosper well during the 1920s as piano markets dwindled.

But by 1933 the country was mired in the Great Depression. The demand for Dominion products had fallen flat. The slow downfall of the company was well described by J.W. Alexander's son, J.B. Alexander, in a 1988 interview conducted by Dan Hoffman, former curator of the Bowmanville Museum.

"You couldn't give pianos away! We went

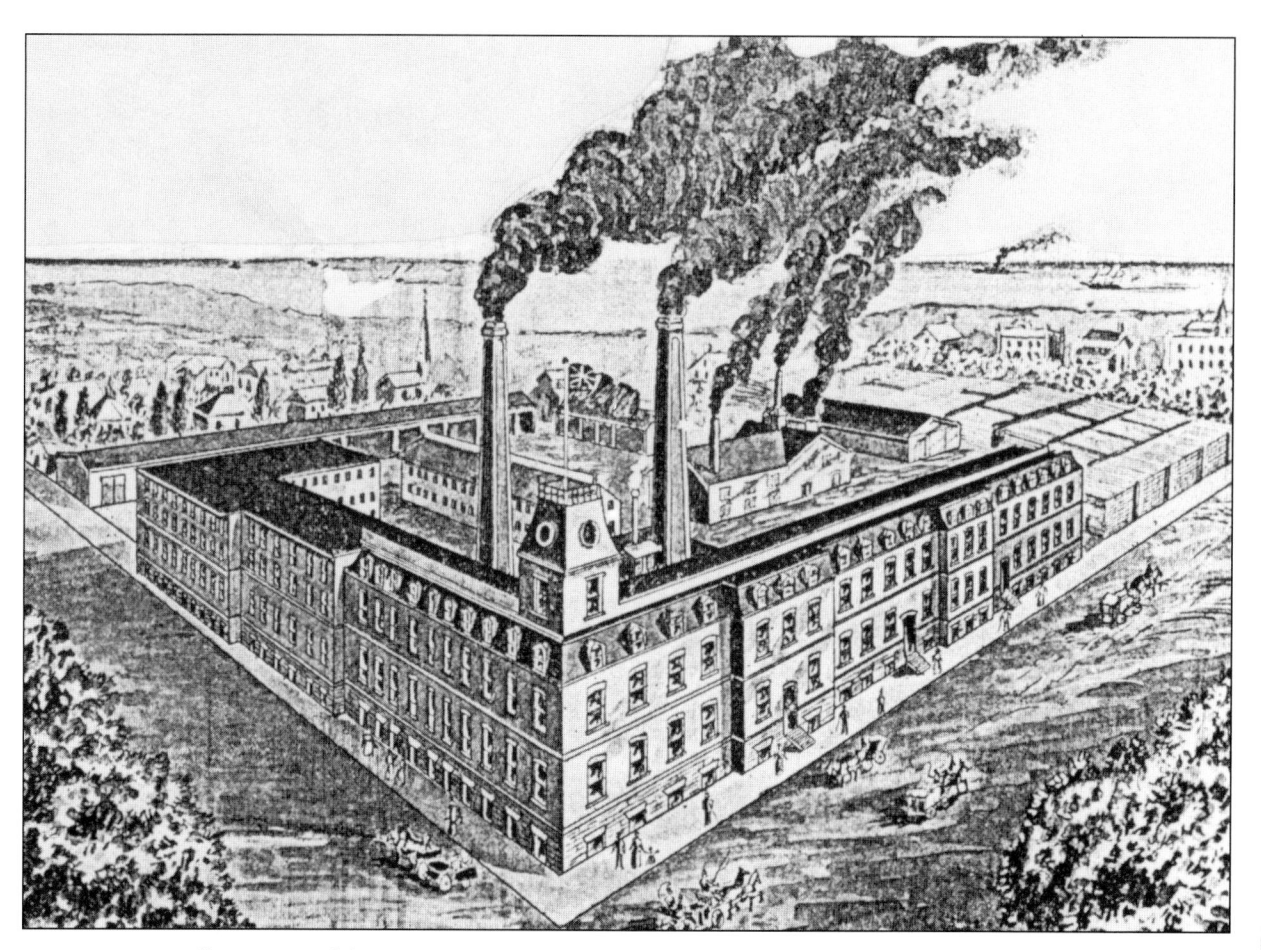

Figure 44. Illustration of the Dominion Organ & Piano Company, c. 1905. In such graphics of the period mountainous billows of smoke were mandatory since they implied productivity and success.

into phonographs ... and they sold very well. But the radio came along and that helped to put the business down. The Williams Piano Company, in Oshawa, tried manufacturing boats. They went out quicker than we did. We thought of amalgamating with a casket manufacturing firm. I remember my father saying "Ach – What a mournful business to be in. Pianos at least bring happiness and entertainment." Motorcar manufacturers would say they [pianos] were probably made too well, pianos didn't depreciate enough to continue the volume."14

That sad commentary echoed through most of the Canadian piano industry in the difficult days of the 1930s. In 1936 Dominion was forced into bankruptcy.

Dominion serial numbers
1890 – 6500   1895 – 7400   1900 – 9000
1905 – 11,500 1910 – 15,700 1915 – 18,000
1920 – 20,000 1923 – 20,500

Figure 45. Ad from the Globe, *13 July 1912.*

Figure 46. Caricature of J.W. Alexander, owner of the Dominion Organ & Piano Company. This cartoon, c. 1910, was appropriate since one of Alexander's chief loves was driving, and being seen in, the latest luxury automobiles.
Note the reference to the Willis Piano Company, one of Dominion's main competitors.

Figure 47. The Dominion Organ & Piano Company band, 1884. Not only is this a unique "cut-out" photo montaged over a drawing, but several aspects of the equipment are notable. Each man sports a canvas bag on his left hip bearing the name "Dominion O & P Co. Band" (see far right) in which he no doubt carried 5" x 7" music cards, a lyre, lubricating oil (for valves & slides), perhaps an extra mouthpiece, and cleaning cloth. From the personal experience of having been a trombonist for five years during the 1960s in one of the last small-town marching bands (and spending countless rehearsal hours with a dozen or more old fellows whose fathers were old enough to tell stories about bands like this), I also note a few other matters that many of us might not perhaps appreciate. That this was a marching band is apparent from the fancy uniforms, which, of course, were provided by the company. The previously mentioned lyre would almost always have been attached (notwithstanding this photo) to each instrument. While these fellows may have loved music, they were factory workers, not professional musicians, and would therefore always march with a music card mounted on the lyre attached to their instruments. The heavy old 48" drums shrank to 30" by the Second World War, but that was too late for the poor fellow in this photograph who carried the drum cum rythmn for a two- or three-mile march in mid-July. The busby-clad band member while usually out front, was generally a cloth-eared, tone-deaf flunky who failed to qualify as a musician but happened to have a reasonable sense of time (and perhaps a father who had drilled military steps into his stride). The real master here is the man in black with cornet in hand. Not marching in step with the uniformed crew, he ran alongside the marching formation hollering "right, left, right foot" instructions, blowing syncopated leads, and hoping that the boys would "do the company (and him) proud" by the end of the parade.

Figure 48. Dominion Organ & Piano Company pavillion at the Canadian National Exhibition, Toronto, c. 1905.

EVANS BROS. PIANO COMPANY LTD.

Two brothers, John and William Evans, opened the doors of a small piano workshop in London in 1872. Producing only a couple of square pianos a month, the modest business managed to survive its first dozen years, but in 1885 E.B. Littler was brought in as a partner. The operation was renamed Evans Bros. and Littler; however, the new partner seemingly did not please John and William Evans. By 1887 Littler was bought out and the Evans boys decided to move the business to the small town of Ingersoll, thirty miles east of London.[15]

While high hopes accompanied the move to larger quarters in a smaller town, Evans Bros. began to fail within the year. By 1889, with several dozen Ingersoll jobs on the line, a consortium of local businessmen – William Watterworth, T. Seldon, Joseph Gibson, W.B. Nelles, the Miller brothers, and David White – stepped in with a rescue package and bought the troubled firm. By 1891 Watterworth was the sole owner, having bought out the other interests.[16]

William Watterworth was born in Ekfrid Township (Middlesex County) on 21 July 1835. A contractor and talented builder by trade, he moved to Ingersoll in 1866 to take up the whole-

Figure 49. The Evans Bros. Piano Manufacturing Company, Ingersoll, Ontario, c. 1892.

sale lumber business. By 1871 Watterworth, who had also become very active in local politics and served as a justice of the peace, had established a thriving furniture manufactory. Later, as president and general manager of the Evans Bros. Piano Manufacturing Company Ltd., Watterworth was responsible for the construction of a large 80' x 60' building at the corner of Thames and St Andrew streets. Always conscious of the opportunity for business growth, Watterworth had expanded the factory by 1905, adding a fourth floor, additional wings, and a power house, lumber-yard, and dry kilns "out back." (See Figures 49 and 50.)

The quality of an Evans piano gained recognition during the 1890s. As the Toronto Mail described it,

> The wood and veneer of which the case is made is carefully selected from air dried material; but to ensure its perfect freedom from moisture it is then twice kiln dried. The iron plate is exceptionally heavy, thus ensuring strength where required. The action, hammers, strings, keys and all other parts are of the very best quality of their respective kinds, and the whole is made up by first-class mechanics, under the careful and constant supervision of Mr. George Brown, a mechanic who has made the construction of the piano his life's work and study, and who is eminently fitted to turn out just an instrument as the public require and demand. The Evans Bros. pianos are noted for their handsome appearance, easy touch, long standing in tune, and for their full, sweet singing tone.[17]

Figure 50. The Evans factory, 1907. It is of interest that the word "Pianoforte" appears on the building. Most companies had dropped the suffix "forte" by at least 1900. Illustration taken from Industrial Ingersoll Illustrated published by the Ingersoll Sun, February 1907.

The same account described the Evans firm as "making preparations to manufacture organs on an extensive scale, and having secured several patents – not at present in use in Canada – which they intend introducing in the construction of these instruments." No documentation could be found to indicate the extent of such activity.

By 1908 Watterworth's son, Kenneth, had worked his way through the company's ranks to become secretary-treasurer and factory manager. William Watterworth retired the next year and the company presidency passed to one Charles White in 1911.

Up to fifty tradesmen were employed at Evans Bros. at the turn of the century, with 400 pianos a year being sold through agents from coast to coast. (Ernest and Sidney Sumner and James Brebner had learned the trade at Evans and struck out on their own to form Sumner & Brebner Pianos in 1906.) While the company was not known as a major piano exporter, at least some of its instruments found their way to South Africa and South America.[18]

An extremely elaborate, solid mahogany Evans Bros. piano of limited edition was manufactured toward the close of the first decade of the new century, receiving honours at the 1910

Chicago World's Fair. (A partial photograph – not suitable for reproduction here – details highly elaborate case carvings and heavy ornamentation on a mahogany mammoth that must have pushed its weight well over 1,000 pounds.) The most popular Evans piano was Style "C", available "in Mahogany or Walnut double veneered inside and out, fully guaranteed for 7 years."[19] Style "M," however, was apparently the firm's "top-of-the-line" model suggested for the serious pianist. A total of eight different models were offered at the company's peak, including a player piano available from 1912.

The Evans Bros. company died a slow death during the 1920s and, like many other Canadian piano manufacturers, ceased operation in the early 1930s. The old Thames St factory that had been built from materials made at the Chas. Jenvey brickyard in nearby Springford was torn down in 1958.[20]

Evans serial numbers
1888 – 5000   1891 – 7000   1895 – 7900
1898 – 8800   1910 – 10,000 1915 – 11,400
1920 – 15,700 1925 – 16,000 1928 – 17,000
(see also Sumner & Brebner)

GERHARD HEINTZMAN COMPANY

Not to be confused with the "other" Heintzman, Theodore Heintzman, the founder of Heintzman & Co., Gerhard Heintzman was Theodore's nephew and established a business separate and distinct from that of his uncle.

Born in Hanover, Germany, on 6 October 1845, Gerhard Heintzman learned the piano trade at the hands of craftsmen in his native land and later in New York. About 1881, however, he had moved to Toronto and established what was to become a thriving Canadian piano business. An 1894 company catalogue – despite its somewhat flowery nature – may best reveal the prominent aspects of Heintzman's early activity. (See Figure 52.)

Although not heavily involved in the export business, Heintzman did manage to have a few branch outlets in Ontario and supplied several dozen large dealers with his lines in cities from Quebec to Manitoba. The Hamilton branch at 128 King St East was managed by Frederick Lunn in 1906, having been established there two years earlier. An account that deals with that store also says that Gerhard Heintzman's Toronto factory produced "two hundred pianos a month and employs 375 men." While the first figure may be correct, the latter must not be, unless, according to comparative figures for other manufacturers of the time, Heintzman's workers were very slow.[21]

The Boudoir Piano.

Styles A and B.

DESCRIPTION:

7 1/3 octave—ivory keys.
Double veneered case.
Overstrung scale.
Three unisons.
Heavy metal plate to top.
Perfect repeating action.
Handsome case with carved legs, engraved or fret panels.
Entire swing front with music rest, also music desk on front fall—continuous hinges on fall.
Height, 4 feet 4 1/2 inches.
Width, 5 feet 2 1/2 inches.
Depth, 2 feet 3 1/2 inches.
Style A—Rosewood finish.
Style B—Natural wood finish in handsome Walnut, Rosewood or Oak veneers.

Figure 51. From the 1894 Gerhard Heintzman catalogue.

MR. GERHARD HEINTZMAN.

A few words by way of Introduction.

IN 1864, some thirty years ago, the subject of this sketch, desirous of becoming a piano maker, though he had then served his time as a worker in wood under careful masters and had earned his certificate as a master workman, voluntarily became an apprentice, his first department of technical study being in the key-making branch of the piano industry in that great centre of musical thought and enterprise, Berlin, Germany.

With a trained knowledge of tools and their use, as well as of woods, veneers and their capabilities, it was not long before advancement, oft-times repeated, rewarded the young student. Still ambition was not satisfied, and ere long we find the young mechanic comparing his skill and the cunning of his brain and hands, with the men of his craft in the new world's Mecca of the piano trade, New York.

Looking backward, it has always been a source of gratification to Mr. Heintzman, that even in this home of the piano industry, he found employment of the highest class the day after his arrival in New York and from that time onward, during the ten years that he followed his craft as journeyman in New York and Canada, he was never without employment; in fact, coming to Toronto for social and family reasons, he spent the greater part of this period as senior foreman of a piano factory and was an important element in the success of the firm with which he was allied.

MR. GERHARD HEINTZMAN.

In 1877, 17 years ago, Mr. Gerhard Heintzman began the manufacture of pianos on his own account, and such had been his training and experience, that the first eight pianos were made entirely by himself; a feat so unique in the history of the Canadian piano industry, that Mr. Heintzman is almost as proud of this, as he is of the fact, that to-day these eight instruments are still in homes where their musical excellence and durability have made life-long friends of the purchasers.

THE GERHARD HEINTZMAN PIANO.

In a word, the enduring qualities of these first pianos indicate the solid foundation on which this enterprise has steadily grown, until to-day there are not eight only, but some four thousand pianos gracing the homes of our professional and amateur pianists, that owe their existence to the skill and enterprise of Mr. Gerhard Heintzman and his staff of workmen.

From 1877 to 1880 Mr. Heintzman manufactured pianos under his own name, the output steadily increasing to meet the demand as the merits of the instruments became known, Mr. Heintzman being joined from time to time by a staff of skilled workmen.

The demand still increasing, additional capital became necessary, so that in 1881 the Heintzman Manufacturing Company was incorporated and a larger output ensued. Business still progressing, overtures were made some years later by a firm of piano dealers to still further augment the capital, which led to the formation of the Lansdowne Piano Co. under letters patent in 1886, with Mr. Gerhard Heintzman as managing director and superintendent of factory. This company, under the personal supervision of Mr. Heintzman, manufactured the instruments then so favorably known as the Lansdowne and the "A. & S. Nordheimer" pianos until 1890, when Mr. Heintzman withdrew from the Company, and with his staff of carefully trained and chosen workmen, together with plant, patterns, materials and all the Lansdowne pianos, finished and under construction, continued his career in the spacious four-story brick factory at 69-75 Sherbourne Street, Toronto, several departments of which are illustrated in the subsequent pages of this catalogue.

The wonderful progress of the business since 1890, and the extraordinary demand for the Gerhard Heintzman piano from the members of the musical profession, and from citizens of refined and artistic taste, are matters so well-known that in concluding this reference to Mr. Heintzman's career, it may be mentioned that plans for the enlargement of the factory are now under consideration. This ever-growing demand, coming from those to whom Mr. Gerhard Heintzman's ability, intelligence and conscientiousness are so well-known, is evidence of the strongest character, that the public are not slow to recognize and reward the manufacturer of trained ability, whose honesty is established and whose motto is, "the highest attainable excellence regardless of labor or cost."

Figure 52. From the 1894 Gerhard Heintzman catalogue.

Figure 53. Ad from the Globe, *23 May 1894.*

Of medium quality, these pianos have apparently not aged well. Many tuners and owners alike have offered less than glowing words about the ability of the Gerhard Heintzman instrument to stay well tuned or to exhibit a bright tone. Exceptions, however, no doubt occur. (Several important patents were granted to Gerhard Heintzman during the years 1882–1900.)

Close to 40,000 instruments were produced by the company until the death of Gerhard Heintzman in 1926. His relatives over at uncle Theodore's took over the line and produced it until 1928. About 1955–59 Quidoz Pianos Ltée used the name Gerhard on one of its lines.

Gerhard Heintzman serial numbers
1893 – 3500   1898 – 5700   1902 – 8400
1906 – 13,000   1909 – 18,500   1913 – 24,000
1919 – 33,000   1925 – 35,000   1927 – 37,500

(Gerhard pianos produced by Quidoz)
1955 – 25,600   1959 – 26,300

HEINTZMAN & COMPANY

In a quiet Berlin music shop, a fourteen-year-old boy worked diligently under the tutorship of his master. Theodor August Heintzmann (1817–99) wanted to make pianos – the best pianos in the world! Heintzmann's employer, Herr Grunow, watched with admiration as his young apprentice applied himself to the pianoforte trade, quickly learning the skills that would help him realize his goal. But one day Theodor apologized to his instructor, threw on his cloak, and walked out the door. There were other matters he needed to know, other talents he needed to acquire.

For several years Heintzmann worked in the instrument, machinist, and cabinet-making trades. At age 27 he married Grunow's daughter, Matilda, and, a few years later, with Prussia and Austria on the brink of war, the Heintzmanns decided that the new world would be a safer place to raise a family. In 1850 they sailed for New York. By coincidence, another Prussian destined to make his mark in the piano business, Heinrich Engelhard Steinweg (later known as Henry Steinway), also arrived in New York that year. Various accounts claim that the two men worked for the New York piano builders Lighte & Newton, but this has not been confirmed.

Heintzmann left New York for Buffalo a couple of years later, spending a year with the Keogh Piano Company and then forming a partnership with two other craftsmen in 1857. The new company, which survived only a year, was known as Drew, Heintzmann and Annowski. Afterwards, at the invitation of Charles Lewis Thomas, founder of Western Piano Manufactory of Canada, Heintzmann moved to Hamilton, Ontario. Working there until 1860, he finally settled in Toronto, finding employment possibly with Charles Thomas' brother, Frank J. Thomas (1862–65). During all these ventures, Theodore Heintzman (as he now spelled his name) kept building instruments of his own in his spare time.

Figure 54. Ad from the Sarnia Observer, 8 December 1922.

A piano design finished in his Toronto kitchen in 1860 is thought to be the one that really launched him on his way. By 1866 he had raised enough capital to open the doors of his own business; he would never work for others again. Two years later his small factory at 105 King Street West was employing twelve workers and turning out sixty pianos a year.22 By 1879 more than 1,000 instruments had been built, with the 2,000 mark being attained by 1884. In 1888 Heintzman opened a new Toronto factory, and production climbed to 1,000 pianos a year.

Figure 56. Heintzman factory, Toronto, c. 1885.

Matilda and Theodore had four sons, each one trained by their father in the ways of the piano business. When Heintzman died in 1899, his youngest son, George, assumed the presidency of Heintzman & Co. An inventive piano craftsman in his own right, George Charles Heintzman had patented several action modifications during the late 1880s and 1890s. (At least three are still on file at the Patent Office, Ottawa.) But his talents as an inventor were no greater than his abilities as a salesman.

With a flair for publicity, George had ridden in 1885 on the cow-catcher of the first transcontinental train to arrive in Vancouver. Swamped by press coverage, he then filled orders for dozens of pianos. At the British and Indian Exhibition the following year, George was in line with dozens of other piano makers vying for awards at the prestigious event. One afternoon, as Queen Victoria strolled down "piano row," all exhibitors stood to attention beside their polished instruments. All, that is, but George. When the queen approached he swung down on the stool and pounded out a tune. The monarch paused to listen. "We didn't realize," she said, "that such beautiful instruments could be made in the colonies." 23

The next afternoon Heintzman and his piano were invited to an audience with the queen. She was pleased. An instrument was sold and arrangements were made to have a Heintzman piano used in a concert at Royal Albert Hall the next day. As workmen hurriedly hoisted the instrument onto the stage an hour before the performance, a foot pedal snapped off. With several thousand patrons watching him, and Queen Victoria waiting an extra half hour in her private salon, sweating George Heintzman, after scrounging for tools, wire, and bits of metal, quickly rigged a reasonable working replacement. The artist performed flawlessly and the monarch was pleased – again. 24

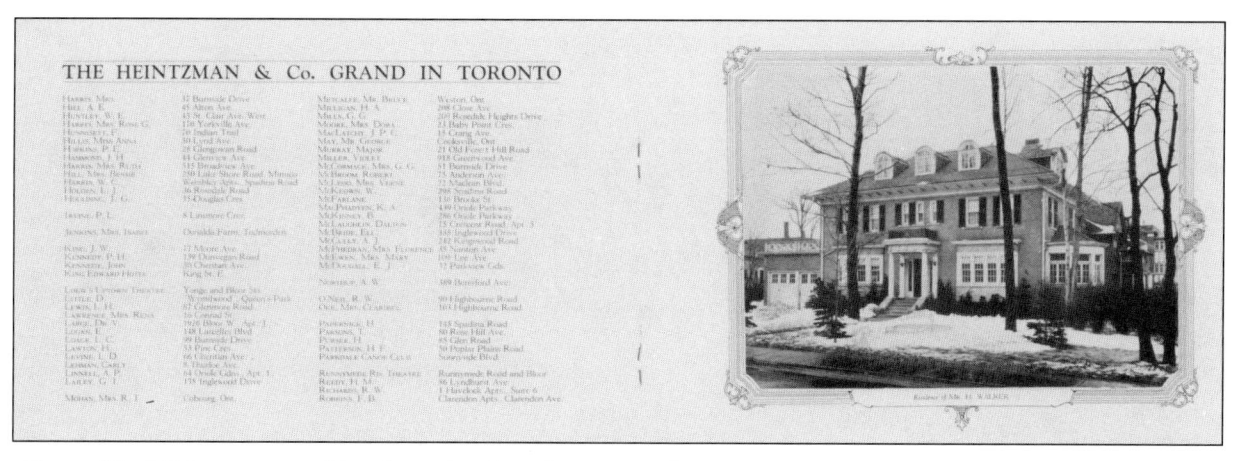

Figure 58. 1923 promotional brochure detailing the names of prominent Toronto citizens, institutions, and artists who endorsed Heintzman grand pianos.

Heintzman's twenty or more stores across the country were often the major retail music centres in Canada's larger cities. Selling not only pianos but all manner of other instruments, accessories, sheet music, records and players – and in the last days furniture and washing-machines – the Heintzman corporation appreciated that diversification was the key to survival.

In the golden days of the early 1920s the Heintzman company, unlike the Steinway approach south of the border, did not pay the great artists to use its instruments exclusively. Instead, the Heintzman philosophy was that its pianos would be judged "on merit alone," and indeed Heintzman instruments did become the preferred choice above every other brand made in Canada. The early view, endorsed by Theodore Heintzman, that the company should make quality instruments, not low-cost items, was a business credo adhered to by Heintzman & Co. for over 120 years. Yet Heintzman was not above mollycoddling itinerant artists. During the heyday of the Canadian piano industry Heintzman instruments were modified and adjusted to suit the whims of whoever happened to be in town. About 1925, Russian pianist Vladimir de Pachmann demanded a keyboard height of 26", not the 28 – 30" standard. With saws in hand, Heintzman workers mutilated the legs of a great black concert grand. De Pachmann tried it out. It wasn't right. What he had really meant was that he liked to play slightly "uphill toward the treble." A one-inch block was shimmed under the right leg. As the last coughs from the audience faded away and de Pachmann sat poised to pounce on the keyboard, he suddenly rose, removed a single sheet of paper from a notepad, and slipped it under a leg of the piano bench. With a contented smile he then sat down and began his concert.

Figure 59. Heintzman price list, 1929.

The Heintzman business no doubt reached a peak in 1922, when there were 400 employees on the payroll and more than 3,000 pianos manufactured in that year alone. Adaptability continued to characterize the company's approach to sales. At its

Figure 60. Heintzman letterhead for its Windsor retail outlet. The store, located at 184 Ouellette Ave., was a prominent Windsor business from 1910 to 1974.

Figure 61. Four Heintzmans with a Heintzman – from left to right, Brad, Herman, George, and William – in 1957.

branch stores almost any household item would be taken in trade. Once, the Windsor store even accepted a horse; unfortunately, to the salesman's chagrin, it dropped dead the next day.

Through the tough days of the Depression Heintzman production dropped to less than 200 pianos a year. But with determination the firm continued to operate. Even in the 1950s and 1960s when television and so many other consumer attractions pushed the piano into the background, Heintzman instruments held a larger portion of the Canadian market than any other piano – domestic or imported.

With four generations of this family having been involved in one way or another in the piano business, the Heintzman saga is truly a story of Canadian determination, versatility, and success. Sadly, the Heintzman piano ceased to be made in the early 1980s.

Heintzman serial numbers

Year	Serial	Year	Serial	Year	Serial
1870	1,400	1880	2,300	1890	7,500
1895	11,000	1900	16,000	1905	24,000
1910	35,000	1915	48,000	1920	61,000
1925	74,000	1930	83,000	1935	84,500
1940	86,400	1945	88,800	1950	93,000
1955	95,000	1960	98,500	1965	112,000
1970	145,000	1975	157,000	1980	164,000

HEINTZMAN PIANOS
NET CASH

VERTICAL PIANOS

Styles	Height	Mahogany	Walnut	Ebonized Bleached Mah. Toasted Mah.	Antique Wal. Limed Oak Special Colors
Elgin	42½"	$890.00	$915.00	$940.00	$965.00
Yorke	42½"	955.00	980.00		1,030.00
Conservatory	50"		985.00		
Royale	44¾"	970.00			
Yorke Louis	42½"	1,030.00	1,055.00		1,195.00

Benches—for above models other than Louis—$25.00
Yorke Louis Bench—$50.00

Normandy Ht. 42½"...... *Antique Wal. only* $1,280.00
Bench—$65.00

GRAND PIANOS

Styles	Length	Mahogany	Walnut
K Miniature	5'3½"	$2,240.00	$2,299.00
D Boudoir	5'10"	2,405.00	2,455.00
G Semi Grand	7'	2,885.00	

Benches—for above models—$25.00
Concert Grand 8'11½"............ $5,035.00 (Ebonized)
Adjustable Artist Bench—$150.00

ART MODELS

Styles	Length	Mahogany	Walnut
K Louis XV	5'3½"	$2,590.00	$2,690.00

Benches—for above models—$55.00
Special designs and finishes to order at slightly additional cost

HEINTZMAN & CO. LIMITED
TORONTO

March 1st, 1953.

NORDHEIMER PIANOS
Product of
HEINTZMAN & CO. LIMITED
NET CASH

VERTICAL PIANOS

Styles	Height	Mahogany	Walnut	Ebonized Bleached Mah. Toasted Mah.	Antique Wal. Limed Oak Special Colors
Minto	41"	$800.00	$825.00	$850.00	$875.00
Minto Louis	41"	875.00	900.00	925.00	950.00
N.3	41"	740.00	765.00		790.00

Bench—for Minto and N.3 models—$25.00
Bench—for Minto Louis model—$50.00

GRAND PIANOS

Styles	Length	Mahogany
Colonial	5'1"	$1,970.00

Bench—for Colonial model—$25.00

Special designs and finishes to order at slightly additional cost

HEINTZMAN & CO. LIMITED
TORONTO

Figure 62. Heintzman price list, 1953. The Nordheimer line of pianos was produced by Heintzman from 1927-64.

D.W. KARN & COMPANY

Dennis Karn was an amateur musician, singing teacher, and instrument maker. During the mid-1860s he had whiled away many evenings tinkering with home-made melodians at his small farm in north Oxford County. In 1867 Karn's love of the instrument had moved him to form a partnership with J.M. Miller who was then manufacturing three or four cabinet reed organs a month for prominent Woodstock citizens. The fledgling firm was called Miller & Karn.

By 1870 Karn, his ambitions outstripping those of Miller, took over the business. The company name was retained until 1873, when D.W. Karn & Company became the new designation. Before long, nine craftsmen were in the employ of Dennis Karn at a small clapboard shop on Dundas St.25 (See Figure 63.) The rapid growth of young industrial Woodstock had created a certain affluence (as countless Victorian mansions in the town still attest today) and thus the market for fine-quality parlour organs and pianos allowed Karn to "push back the walls." A move to larger quarters on Dundas St. West seemed appropriate; however, fire levelled the operation in the spring of 1879. Karn rebuilt. But disaster struck again in 1886 when the entire factory was once again razed to the ground.26 Many men would have been crushed from such a calamity, but not Dennis Karn. Even though he had been physically slowed down by his recent involvement in a passenger train accident, he put his face to the wind and built up what was to be the largest industry in Woodstock.

After the 1886 fire, Karn quickly acquired the financially troubled Woodstock hotel, added a large addition to it to accommodate his organ works, and bought a large parcel of land across the street where an incredible 300' x 90' four-storey brick structure was built to serve as the piano department of the company. *The Woodstock Evening Sentinel-Review* of 17 May 1897 describes the operation as containing "the latest and most modern impro-vements in woodworking and labour saving machines; it stands unrivalled for completeness and thoroughness of equipment." With a large lumber yard, drying barns and kilns, an oil and varnish factory, large boilers, steam engines, elevators, automatic sprinklers, miles of steam and gas pipes, and its own fire brigade as well as several rail sidings, the Karn factory was truly a "city within a city."

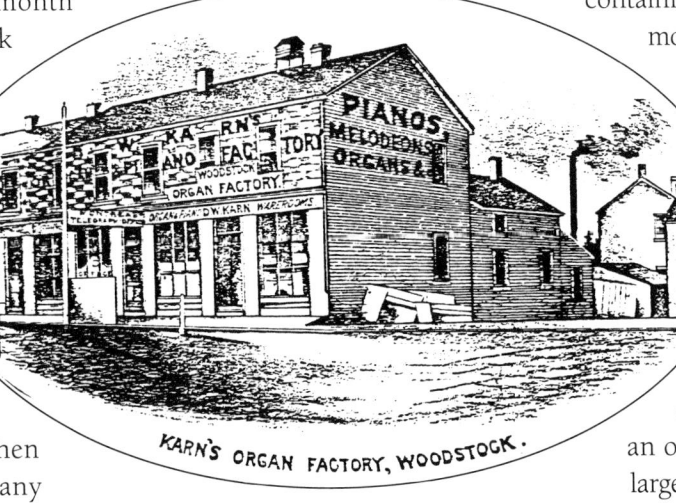

Figure 63. Drawing from The Historical Atlas Of Oxford County, *1876.*

But the sweet smell of success, sawdust, and shellac were not the only things that appealed to Karn. He was elected mayor of Woodstock in 1889 and ran twice, though unsuccessfully, for the provincial legislature.

Karn was meticulous when it came to the finished product. Each of the manufactured instruments that left his factory carried a comprehensive seven-year warranty. By 1898, 150 organs and 25 pianos a week were being turned out by 250 workmen who took home better than $9,000 in wages each month. Karn employees seemed very well treated and content by industrial standards of the day and could boast at producing instruments of exceptional quality which were praised world-wide. A September 1889 issue of the *Sentinel-Review* gave a glowing report:

> *The single aim and motto of the firm has been to make the Karn Organ the best in the world. No imitation can be found in these instruments, the wood being black walnut, and its construction such as to ensure long wear. Their goods are made first-class. The designs are chaste, action is perfect, and the finish is such as to command the highest admiration. This firm makes over 75 styles of organs, from an instrument with only one set of reeds to one with 18 sets. The fact that these instruments are being largely sold and supplied in Germany and Switzerland, the home of music and musicians, only goes to prove the superiority of the Karn Organ.*

Priced from $30 – $60 in the early 1890s, and sold on easy terms, Karn organs and pianos were available to families of even modest means. Dozens of Karn instruments were supplied to public schools in Japan at the turn of the century, And with scores of awards, medals, and trade show diplomas, Karn keyboards were fondled in every part of the world. Borrowing from an old adage, the Toronto *Mail* of 13 September 1888 proudly stated that "the sun never goes down upon the Karn Organ!" There were branch outlets exisitng in major cities from coast to coast and also in London, England, and Hamburg, Germany.

In 1896, with product lines still expanding, Karn bought the rights to produce a line of reed organs made by the S. R. Warren Company of Toronto. Soon the Karn-Warren pipe organ began to appear in newspaper ads. (The Warren company apparently moved to Woodstock sometime prior to the First World War and in 1921 sought a $30,000 municipal loan, claiming that it would be able to generate $75,000 a year in wages, commercial benefits, and tax revenue for the citizens

Figure 64. Picture of Dennis W. Karn taken by Woodstock photographer A.G. Westlake, c. 1898.

Figure 65. Employees of the Karn Organ & Piano Company prepare for an industrial parade in Woodstock, c. 1900.

of Woodstock. The company was then specializing in the building of theatre organs; one of its instruments found a home at Toronto's Imperial Theatre and was described by the press in 1920 as "the largest pipe organ ever installed in a Canadian theatre.")

Musical fads and inventions necessitated continous product changes. In 1906 the Karn company turned out a line of player pianos – a product that won it national acclaim – and in later years also produced gramophone cabinets and a series of music-disk machines called "Regina Coronas."

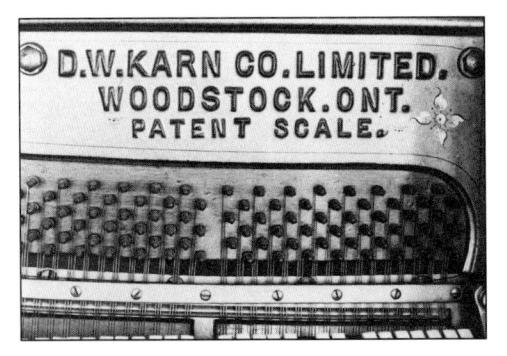

Figure 66. Interior of an 1896 Karn piano. Note the hand-painted floral designs and pin striping.

After Dennis Karn retired in 1909, the company entered a business arrangement with Morris Pianos of Listowel, Ontario. The new firm, Karn-Morris Piano and Organ Company, made several models at both the Woodstock and Listowel factories until the partnership was dissolved in 1920. At that time the remaining Karn assets were picked up jointly by the Cecilian Piano Company and Sterling Action and Keys, Ltd., both of Toronto. However, this new venture was also quite short-lived and failed by 1924. Sherlock-Manning then bought all remaining assets and continued to produce a Karn-name piano until 1961.

Much of the old Karn factory, which had seen various other manufacturers and tenants come and go, was destroyed by fire on 10 November 1961.[27]

About 1920, when the demise of the Karn Company was in sight, a number of employees banded together to form the Woodstock Organ Company. Headed by designer T. J. Palmer, the firm manufactured pipe organs and, according to a sales list on file at the Woodstock Public Library, installed them in 147 churches across Canada. When this company failed in the late 1920s, the average cost of its instrument was $25,000, with an on-site installation time of six months. A subsequent firm, Woodstock Pipe Organ Builders, was extant from 1935 to 1955.

Karn Serial Numbers
1890 – 1,000   1895 – 3,000   1900 – 4,700
1905 – 7,400   1907 – 8,900   1910 – 10,000
1915 – 13,000
(The *Pierce Piano Atlas* lists several numbers 1936-61)
(see also Morris Piano Company)

Figure 67. A typical Karn organ, c. 1885. Thousands of these organs were exported all over the globe.

LESAGE PIANOS LTD.
(LES PIANOS LESAGE LTÉE)

As sap began flowing up the maples in the early spring of 1891, a sweet idea was coursing through the mind of a farmer from Ste-Thérèse-de-Blainville. Damase Lesage had always loved music, but his farm life and a stint on a Quebec line of Canadian Pacific Railways had not allowed him to pursue his love.

On 13 March 1891, however, with money in hand from the sale of one of his farms, Lesage walked into the office of the troubled Canadian Piano Company, laid $10,000 on the table, and bought himself a business.

His wife, Isabella, and his neighbours cheered him on as Lesage methodically dismantled the piano firm that had been started in Ste-Thérèse by Thomas F. G. Foisy just a few years earlier. Examining each aspect of the business – the skilled workforce, the supply of materials, marketing, and sales – Demase Lesage slowly built up a company that would last for almost 100 years.

Less than a year into the new venture, Lesage realized that his expertise behind the plow would not help him behind the piano. So an associate named Procule Piché, who had spent a number of years in the trade, was taken on as a partner, the firm now being called Lesage & Piché. Employing a number of the craftsmen from the old Foisy company, the new business now began to make headway. By the early 1900s production at the Ste-Thérèse plant had reached 500 instruments a year. By 1904 Piché had left the business. In that year Lesage's son Adélard, who had been at his father's side from the beginning, began shouldering much of the load in the family business. Renamed Lesage & Fils, the company continued to grow rapidly and was the major supplier of name pianos for C. W. Lindsay Company and Willis Pianos Ltd., both of Montreal.

The Willis firm, however, was eager to be in the piano manufacturing business and subse-

Figure 68. The Lesage factory, Ste-Thérèse-de-Blainville, c. 1978.

quently bought a controlling interest in Lesage in 1907. But by 1911 Adélard was displeased with the relationship, sold his remaining shares to Willis, and, with the help of his own sons, Jacques-Paul and Jules (and later Gérard), put the Lesage name and company back in the family.

Production figures rose steadily as the company expanded its factory in 1916 and again in 1926, at which time over 2,000 pianos a year were waltzing out their doors. Wielding such financial influence and piano power, they took over Craig Piano Co., Montreal, in 1930, Bell Piano & Organ Co., Guelph, in 1934, and Kinston's Weber Piano Co. in 1939 – and all of this in a decade that had spelled the end for many of the piano concerns of Canada.

With company mottos such as "Now is the time to think positive" and "Second to none," this courageous family enterprise continued to broaden its horizons. After 1942, when its name changed to Lesage Pianos Ltd., the export doors to Australia, New Zealand, Europe, South America, and the Caribbean were opened wide.[28]

During the 1950s and 1960s slower, but steady, activity continued at the 45,000-square-foot Lesage plant. (A total of 30,000 instruments had been made by 1950.)[29] There were fewer and fewer domestic competitors, the main challenge now coming from Japanese and Korean imports. More lax tariff restrictions and a growing "couldn't-care-less" attitude on the part of all levels of government, meant that by the 1970s Lesage, like its few remaining Canadian counterparts, began to feel seriously threatened.

A brief turn to electronic keyboards in the late 1970s, and new blood in the form of Gérard Lesage's son, Jacques, representing the fourth generation to enter the trade, did not bring the anticipated results. With sixty people still on the

Figure 69. Lesage workers long took pride in their skill as piano mechanics. Through the brilliance of Gérard Lesage, many machines used on their production lines were inventions unique to the industry. This particular device was used to drill tuning-pin holes in such a precise way that even tension of all tuning pins was achieved.

Figure 70. Photos of Adélard Lesage, Gérard Lesage and Paul Lesage from a company brochure c. 1982.

Figure 71. The Lesage 5' 3" baby grand. Manufactured from 1981-86 this model was available in oak, walnut, cherrywood, teak, or ebony finish. With a twenty-five year warranty and some unique technical features, it was truly a great Canadian piano. (Sadly, the notion of a "twenty-five year warranty" evaporated with the demise of Lesage in late 1986.)

Figure 72. A contemporary piano produced by Lesage shortly before the company failed in 1986.

Figure 73. The Lesage "Versailles" model. Popularized versions of this compact, drop-action piano were the "stock-in-trade" for Lesage, Heintzman, Sherlock-Manning, and Willis from the mid-1950s onward. This Lesage was 41" high and carried a twenty-five year guarantee against any splitting on the sounding board.

payroll in 1979, something had to be done. The export trade for Canadian pianos had fallen off for several decades, but an attempt was made to have a crack at the international nut again. In 1981 Lesage reintroduced its grand piano, which had been out of production for twenty years, and with a capital of $75,000 the company tried to market this product in Europe.[30]

The effort and capital seemed to be the good chasing the bad, as the company had little success on the European stage. By mid-1986 the Royal Bank of Canada had called all its notes.[31] The sweet tones from Lesage had reached the last bar.

Apart from the names of Craig, Bell, Mendelssohn, Schuman, Belmont, and Weber that the Lesage firm had acquired by means of takeover, the names Sonata, Continental Euro, Anniversary, Minuet, Concerto, Concord Canadian, Prelude, Versailles: French Provincial, and Versailles: Queen Anne were used by Lesage.

Of all piano serial numbers in Canada, Lesage's have been perhaps the best recorded. They are as follows:

1895 – 1,000	1900 – 2,100	1905 – 5,000
1910 – 8,200	1915 – 11,000	1920 – 15,300
1925 – 18,600	1930 – 21,500	1935 – 24,000
1940 – 26,400	1945 – 28,300	1950 – 30,500
1955 – 33,400	1960 – 36,000	1965 – 42,000
1970 – 50,000	1975 – 56,000	1980 – 64,000
1985 – 67,300		

MASON & RISCH

Founded in 1871, this notable Canadian piano firm would survive for more than 100 years. As an accountant for Norheimers, Thomas Gabriel Mason wondered why that company was content to import all its pianos from the United States. With careful planning and a few intelligent piano designs registered in the patent office, Mason stepped out on his own.

A close friend, Vincent Risch, and Octavius Newcombe had similar wide-eyed dreams of starting their own business. Together with Mason they formed a partnership and opened a retail outlet. During their early years they, too, were just distributors of other popular pianos, but by 1877 a few of their own instruments were being built in a small Toronto workshop. The following year, Newcombe, content with the experience gained, decided that he would launch out on his own. At age thirty-two he formed a company that would soon rival that of his two friends.

During the period 1886-90 Mason, Risch, and Newcombe entered into a brief business venture with Albert and Samuel Nordheimer and Gerhard Heintzman. The Lansdowne Piano Company was formed in Toronto, producing name pianos for each of their respective operations. Heintzman had emerged as the dominant character by 1890, the alliance dissolved, and each moved on to develop its own piano business. Robert Gourlay had apparently been involved in this firm as well. He is shown as a co-signer on a Mason patent registration for 1886. (For more details see Gourlay, Winter and Leeming; Gerhard Heintzman; Newcombe Piano Company; and Nordheimer Piano and Music Company)

From 1891 onward Mason & Risch thundered onto the Canadian piano market. Establishing retail instrument and music stores in several dozen cities from coast to coast, and later selling records and players, the company became a giant in the music trade. One of the major coups for Mason & Risch was its perennial contract with the T. Eaton Company. From the days of the First World War until the demise of the firm in the 1970s, the large national department store carried several Mason & Risch instruments in each retail outlet and included them in its massive semi-annual catalogues. Most of the Eaton name pianos distributed were contract items manufactured by Mason & Risch.

By 1950 total sales figures had climbed to 65,000 units. the firm was taken over by Winter

Figure 74. Ad from the Globe, 2 July 1904.

& Co. (New York) about that time and the national retail network was dropped.[32] Quality fell badly from the mid-1950s although sales figures do not seem to have suffered comparatively. In the late 1960s a lumber mill in Woodstock, New Brunswick, was purchased to provide the Toronto factory with specific cabinet and case components. Matt Willis, formerly of Willis & Co., was national sales manager with Mason & Risch during 1968-69. In a 1989 interview he was asked what the instrument quality was like in those late days of Mason & Risch. With a gentlemanly air Matt rolled his eyes and shook his head. The company closed about 1972.

Mason & Risch serial numbers
1891 – 5,000   1896 – 8,500   1900 – 11,000
1905 – 14,000 1910 – 23,000 1915 – 31,000
1925 – 41,000 1935 – 51,000 1945 – 57,000
1950 – 70,000 1955 – 81,000 1960 – 103,000
1965 – 130,000 1970 – 152,000

MORRIS, FEILD & ROGERS COMPANY

On 18 July 1890 one of the most important businesses in the small town of Listowel, Ontario, declared bankruptcy. The Hess, Hess & Rosbach Furniture Company had turned its last chair leg, varnished its last oak table. As scores of workers faced the prospect of a gloomy fall and winter, the Listowel town council stepped in with a rescue package designed to save jobs and ensure the community's future.

A brief flurry of activity under a new name saw the furniture plant back in high gear by the end of 1891, only to fall flat within four months. Enter three local businessmen, Morris, Feild, and Rogers, and an idea that promised an end ot Listowel's unemployment woes.

"Why not start a piano factory? It's easy! We have the furniture plant and the knowhow to make piano cases and stools. We'll just hire someone to fill them with strings and hammers and things like that!" (This scenario was common in the Canadian piano industry. Many firms got their start under such circumstances and were little more than furniture makers which assembled pre-manufactured piano components. By hiring one or two real piano industry experts, these firms could overcome most technical difficulties.)

It seemed to good to be true. But then, successful businesses have been built on poorer foundations than that.

The Listowel triumvirate succeeded in wooing several piano industry people from the defunct Brantford Piano Company and by late 1892 sweet notes were issuing from the old Hess furniture building.33

The Morris, Feild and Rogers Piano Company survived for a dozen years. The early boom days of the new century witnessed the export of thousands of Listowel-made instruments to every corner of Canada and even to Europe. But by 1904 the trio of entrepreneurs were at loggerheads concerning the future direction of the firm. The partnership was dissolved and Morris became the principal shareholder in a firm now reorganized as Morris Piano Co. Ltd.

New blood, in the form of J.W. Scott (vice-president) and E.C. Thornton (general manager), was brought in. The *Listowel Banner* happily reported on 5 February 1904 that "all shareholders appear to believe that Mr. E.C. Thornton is well qualified as manager of our factory." Business continued to look rosy until an early morning fire on 10 October 1908, gutted the whole operation causing damage estimated at $75,000. Sixty men were suddenly out on the street; local merchants moaned. The weekly payroll from the factory had been a whopping $600. What now?

Figure 75. Some of the Morris staff, c. 1922. Lou Burrows (standing) was factory manager; others unknown.

Like a benevolent father, town council once again entered the scene with a $25,000 pledge to rebuild the factory. But this wasn't enough even when added to the private capital Morris raised. By the end of the year the picture was still cloudy. Whispers of permanent closure sifted through the local rumour mills.[34]

Undaunted by the dismal prospects, the Morris corporate heads looked for outside help and found it. By early 1909 Morris shareholders were actively courting Woodstock piano magnate Dennis Karn. When March arrived the new firm Morris and Karn Piano & Organ Company Ltd., supposedly bankrolled by Karn to the tune of $1 million, unfurled its banner. The town of Listowel was at peace again. With D.W. Karn as the new president, W. R. Tudhope, vice-president, and E.C. Thornton remaining as general manager, the company entered a most propsperous phase.

"The company expects to employ 150 hands beginning the first of May with an output of 200 pianos per year," trumpeted the local press. And indeed such optimistic forecasts were realized. By 1914 regular export shipments were being made to New Zealand and Australia; whole boxcars of Morris and Karn pianos rolled down the rails destined for Halifax and Vancouver. But during the dark days of the Great War, Morris & Karn, like so many of its contemporaries, moved to rallentando. The finale came on 14 March 1924 at the company's last annual meeting. "We have decided to cease operations when the present supply of

Figure 76. The boiler room at the Morris piano factory c. 1922. Stationary engineer Charlie "Felty" Keeso (left) and boiler expert John Nathaniel Baker, formerly from Burford, Ontario.

.music for W. H. Penn's song, There's Nobody Just Like You, also carried the famous slogan of the Morris company—There's merit in the "Morris".

Morris Pianos

One Grade only and that the Highest.
They combine more scientfic improvements than any other Piano.
Pianos sold on Easy Terms of payment.

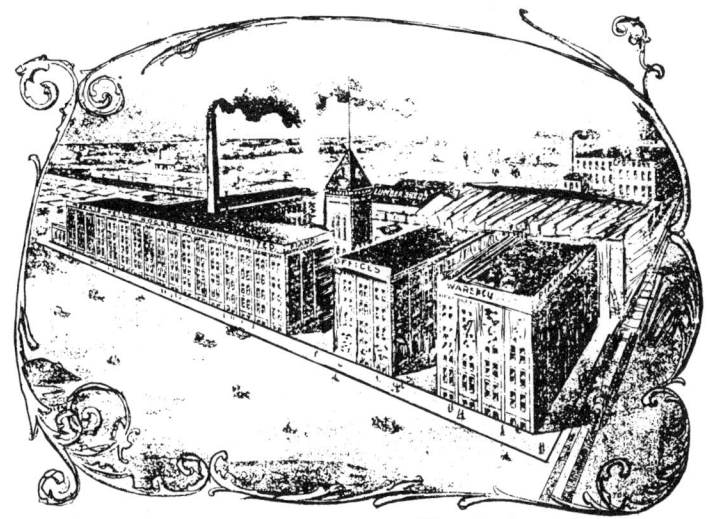

The most modern and finest equipped Piano Factory in Canada.

MORRIS PIANOS

Chaste in Design   Elegantly Finished
Unexcelled in Workmanship   Even Scale
Sympathetic Touch   Prompt in Repetition

Guaranteed for an unlimited length of time by a responsible Company.

Write for Catalogue and Prices.

The Morris Piano Co., Limited
LISTOWEL, ONT.

Toronto Warerooms, 276 Yonge St.   Winnipeg, 228 Portage Ave.

Figure 77. Ad from the Listowel Banner, c. 1905.

actions is exhausted and, if possible, dispose of the plant. Members of the firm are frank in the statement that our handicap has been financial, since we posess both the equipment, facilities and knowhow to produce one of the finest pianos in the Dominion."[35]

A brief revival for an eighteen month period from October 1926 occurred when the International Piano Company attempted to use the Listowel facilities as a branch of its Toronto operation. But by the spring of 1928 the end was certain. Ironically, the buildings that had housed the Morris piano business for more than thirty years were next occupied by the Listowel Casket Company.

Morris serial numbers
Morris, Feild & Rogers
1892 –   1893 – 2,000   1894 – 3,500
1895 – 6,000 1897 – 7,500   1900 – 8,000
1902 – 9,000

Morris Piano Co. Ltd.
1904 – 9,500 1906 – 10,000 1908 – 11,000

Morris & Karn Organ & Piano Company
1909 – 12,000 1912 – 13,5000 1914 – 15,000
1916 – 17,000 1920 – 18,000   1922 – 19,000
1924 –

Figure 78. The Morris piano factory, Listowel, Ontario, c. 1930.

NEWCOMBE PIANO COMPANY

An inventive Englishman, Octavius Newcombe started this company in 1878 at age thirty-two. Having previously gained experience in the piano trade with Tom Mason and Vincent Risch (later Mason & Risch), Newcombe had formed a partnership with the pair back in 1871. One year after the founding of his own company Octavius Newcombe took on his brother, Henry, as a partner. Building square pianos (until c. 1881), grands, and uprights, they patented several clever inventions and won wide acclaim for their upright models in particular. An award at the World Industrial and Cotton Centennial Exposition in New Orleans in 1884 and a medal and diploma received two years later at a major exhibition in London, England, gave the young company the confidence and clout to enter the export trade.[36]

The quality of the Newcombe instruments was further praised by Sir Arthur Sullivan (of Gilbert & Sullivan fame), who selected a Newcombe piano for the use of Queen Victoria at Windsor Castle.[37]

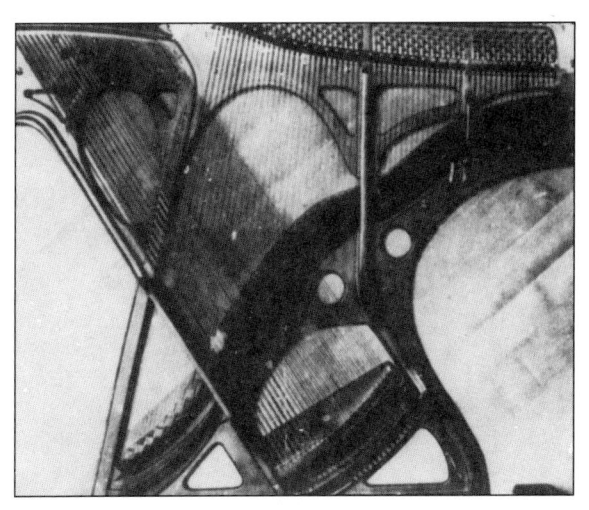

Figure 79. An interesting upright iron plate for which Octavius and Henry Newcombe received industrial design protection in April 1896.

Figure 80. The cover of a 1903 Newcombe brochure.

When fire destroyed the five-storey Newcombe factory in 1926, manufacturing ceased, although Henry carried on as a retailer into the mid-1930s. (Octavius Newcombe had died about 1905.) The rights to the company name were bought by Albert Willis, who manufactured a Newcombe piano until 1960. (See also Lansdowne Piano Company.)

Newcombe serial numbers
1878 – 1,600   1886 – 2,100   1892 – 2,900
1896 – 4,000   1900 – 5,500   1905 – 9,500
1907 – 11,500 1913 – 14,000 1918 – 20,000

NORDHEIMER PIANO & MUSIC COMPANY

Billing themselves as "the oldest piano company in the Dominion," the Nordheimer brand name was indeed the longest lasting in Canadian music history.[38] In June 1844, brothers Samuel and Abraham Nordheimer opened a small shop at 122 King St. East, Toronto, offering music books, square pianofortes, and sewing supplies. As an agent for Broadwood, Stodert and Chickering instruments, the firm did not actually enter the piano manufacturing business until 1886.

By that year Samuel and Albert (Abraham's son) had decided that the piano retail trade was just too lucrative for them to remain simply as agents. Forming a partnership with Gerhard Heintzman, the Nordheimers opened the Lansdowne Piano Company. Tom Mason, Vincent Risch, and Octavius Newcombe were also connected with this venture, each having his own brand name stencilled on the pianos that came down the Lansdowne line.

The strong figure in the corporation was apparently Gerhard Heintzman. When his ambitions grew greater than those of his partners in 1890, they separated and went their respective ways. Albert and Uncle Samuel were disappointed by the split but determined to press on. They built their own factory in east Toronto and began turning out one of the finer pianos made in Canada. With its instruments of enduring quality

Figure 81. Ad from the Globe, *3 June 1844.*

Figure 82. Illustration from the Nordheimer Music Book of 1904.

receiving dozens of awards, the Nordheimer Piano & Music Company opened branch outlets in Winnipeg, Montreal, Quebec, and a half dozen Ontario centres. Their three-storey shop in Hamilton, which opened 30 April 1907, was described in the local press as one of "the most complete and up-to-date piano and music houses" in North America.[39]

As a manufacturer of grands, uprights, and player pianos, Nordheimer had produced 11,000 instruments by 1910 and 21,500 by 1921.[40] When old Samuel Nordheimer died in 1912 at age ninety, his estate was valued at more than $1.5 million. In his generosity he had willed many thousands of dollars to benevolent societies, hospitals, servants and former employees. His son, Roy, and three daughters shared the bulk of the will, which included the explicit instruction that they mantain Samuel's beloved Toronto residence, Glenedyth.[41]

With the retirement of Albert Nordheimer in 1927, Heintzman & Company bought the factory and carried on the Nordheimer line until the mid-1960s.

Nordheimer serial numbers
1890 – 2,500	1895 – 3,800	1900 – 5,550
1905 – 7,500	1910 – 11,000	1915 – 15,000
1920 – 18,000	1925 – 21,000	1930 – 22,000
1935 – 22,300	1940 – 23,000	1945 – 24,000
1950 – 25,000	1955 – 25,6000	1960 – 27,800

Figure 83. Ad from the Globe, *13 June 1912.*

SHERLOCK-MANNING PIANOS LTD.

When Messrs J. Frank Sherlock and Wilber N. Manning organized the Sherlock-Manning Piano and Organ Co. thirteen years ago on a certain Friday (Nov. 13, 1902), they showed a splendid disregard for the hoodo supposedly attached to this particular day in the week. Certainly this organization effected on Friday (the 13th) has had a continued record of business progress. Since that day they have manufactured and sold 30,000 instruments, so built and governed by such marketing policies that the house's reputation for square dealing, and the reputation of its pianos, has extended, not only into every nook and corner in Canada, but to all parts of the English speaking world.
– *Canadian Music Trades Journal,*
15 March 1915.

J. Frank Sherlock and Wilber N. Manning had started in the piano trade as Doherty employees in Clinton, Ontario, in 1890. On Friday, 13 November 1902, however, they decided to leave Clinton behind and establish their own business in London, sixty miles to the south. Within two years the Sherlock-Manning Organ Co. was manufacturing 100 organs a month and employing 60 workers.

Since the demise of the reed organ was imminent, the pair changed the name of their firm to Sherlock-Manning Piano and Organ Co. in 1910, although actual piano production appears to have started in May 1903. An active salesman, Frank Sherlock wrote orders from coast to coast and established a roaring export trade with Australia, New Zealand, Great Britain, China, Japan, South Africa, the West Indies, and South America. In 1920 Sherlock and Manning had sufficient capital to buy out their old boss, Doherty. Within the next four years expansion and takeover were their watchwords. By 1925 they had acquired Haines Bros., Marshall & Wendell, Foster-Armstrong, Gourlay, Winter & Lemming, and Karn.[42]

Employing women in almost every department as early as 1915, Sherlock-Manning was the first piano company in Canada to pay male and female workers equal wages for similar types of work. (In fact, although many piano firms had failed to appreciate it, women – with smaller hands – were often better suited to working with delicate piano actions than their clumsy, big-pawed male counterparts.)

Manufacturing organs, players, uprights, and grands, Sherlock-Manning offered several dozen models and variations in their annual catalogue. As head of the Canadian Piano and Organ Manufacturers Association in 1924, Wilber

Figure 84. The Sherlock-Manning plant in London prior to its purchase of Doherty Piano & Organ Co. All operations were eventually moved to the Clinton factory. This is a portion of an ad originally run in the Farmer's Advocate, *1 March 1917.*

Figure 85. The Sherlock-Manning factory, Clinton, c. 1945. By this time the rail spur that had once passed between the two buildings had been torn up. The two men standing in the doorway are Caryl Draper and Bert Gibbings. As there are no vehicles in sight it would seem that this picture was taken on a Sunday or holiday.

Manning understood the importance of offering variety to the consumer. That same year the company was renamed Sherlock-Manning Pianos Ltd.

Both owners had introduced family into the trade. G.W. and A.E. Sherlock, sons of Frank Sherlock, had been brought through the ranks as had H.B. Manning, a nephew of Wilber Manning, who entered the firm as a capable accountant.[43]

By 1930, when the company still enjoyed strong sales both inside and outside Canada, old age had overtaken Sherlock and Manning. Frank Sherlock died in 1931 and Wilber Manning in January 1935. Former vice-president Addison A. Pegg (who had learned the business at Nordheimer's), then took control with Caryl Draper becoming the new vice-president. The reorganized company was fully in place by 1 July 1936.

During the difficult days to follow, diversity was seen as essential to keeping the Clinton factory "in the black." An experiment with an electric organ was tried in the early 1940s as was contract manufacturing of organ and radio cabinets, wooden radar cases for the navy, and even outdoor bowling alleys and shuffleboards. Anything to keep the company afloat! Additionally, a compact English piano, known as the "Minx," was regarded as a panacea that would rescue Sherlock-Manning from its economic ills. The idea – instead of a blessing – was a financial disaster. (See also "Minx" in the section The Pianos of Canada: A to Z.)

As sales declined, Caryl Draper, one of the most talented craftsmen in the piano industry of the time, was largely responsible for the development of the drop action, compact (apartment-size) piano. Working with some of the design ideas used in the "Minx" and drawing upon his earlier experiments from the mid-1920s, Draper finally developed an acceptable, fine quality 41" high piano. The remaining major companies of the day – Willis, Lesage, Heintzman, and Mason & Risch – were quick to design and offer similar products from the early 1950s onward.[44]

On the death of Addison Pegg in 1958, his son Dudley became president until the company was taken over by Bill Heintzman in 1967. Caryl Draper died in 1968, passing on his shares of the business to his two sons, Murray and Bob.

During the 1970s, the decade that witnessed the final act in the saga of the Canadian piano industry, Bill Heintzman had to devote more attention to his earlier love, Heintzman & Company. As a result, Murray and Bob Draper, along with office manager Joe Reid, bought the controlling interests in 1978 in a last-ditch effort to save Sherlock-Manning and the thirty-six jobs that were on the line. The new firm, Draper Bros. & Reid, succeeded in keeping the saws turning for a few years. But in 1984, when a group of Toronto businessmen showed interest in purchasing the factory, the offer seemed too good to refuse.[45]

From 1985 to 1988, despite valiant efforts, several ownership changes, and absolutely no help from any level of government, the once great Sherlock-Manning Piano Company – the last piano business in Canada – gasped its last breath and fell silent.

Sherlock-Manning serial numbers
1905 – 5,000   1910 – 10,000   1915 – 14,000
1920 – 90,000   1925 – 97,000   1930 – 101,000
1935 – 105,000 1940 – 108,000 1945 – 110,000
1950 – 114,000 1955 – 117,000 1960 – 120,000
1965 – 123,000 1970 – 127,000 1975 – 131,000
1980 – 164,000 1985 – 235,000

Figure 86. Sherlock-Manning model SM-15000A, 52" high, c. 1979. This was the last of the large style uprights to be made in Canada.

Figure 87. Sherlock-Manning model #6000W, manufactured c. 1970-87.

Sherlock-Manning Canada
SINCE 1875

Yes, since 1875, Sherlock-Manning pianos have been bringing sound enjoyment to thousands, both in Canada, and abroad. In fact Sherlock-Manning is the oldest, continually operated Piano Manufacturer in Canada. Where once hundreds flourished, now, few have survived. In all of North America, there remains only a dozen piano manufacturers; three in all of Canada.

In the highly technical world of mass production, it gives us a great deal of satisfaction and pride to produce a totally hand made piano. Each piano is painstakingly crafted from the finest of Canadian and European woods, with the greatest attention to detail.

Our sounding boards are constructed of solid spruce (not laminated), crowned for tension and tapered at the edges for greater resonance and tonal vibration. Hard maple graduated ribs are carefully placed to maintain crown and ensure correct tonal transmissions.

Six solid maple posts, ensure maximum strength and greater resistance to climatic changes.

Perhaps the greatest single element in maintaining tune and ensuring years of quality performance, is the construction of the Tuning Pin Block. The Sherlock-Manning pin block is constructed of twelve ply cross grained delignit, laminated to a hardwood maple back, into which the tuning pins are anchored. What all of this means, is that there is less chance of pin slippage, resulting in a piano that stays in tune longer and requires less service.

What you feel when you play a Sherlock-Manning piano, is a smooth responsive touch, which is a result of the superior quality of the "action". The action in a Sherlock-Manning piano is hand lifted, spaced and balanced after being aligned individually to the strings. Genuine buck-skin is used on the butt cushions, giving a greater feeling of control and response.

Another area where Sherlock-Manning stands uniquely superior, is the design of the bass to treble scale. The copper wound strings in the bass scale extend four notes into the treble scale, softening the transition from bass to treble. This is a relatively simple idea, but then most good ideas are. There are many reasons for buying a Sherlock-Manning piano, however we feel that you should only remember two —

FIRST . . . we're Canadian   SECOND . . . to none!

Figure 88. A Sherlock-Manning promotional brochure produced by company owners Draper Bros. & Reid Ltd., c. 1979.

WEBER PIANO COMPANY LTD. and WORMWITH PIANO COMPANY LTD.

Since the activities of the Weber and Wormwith companies in Kingston were inseparably intertwined, their stories are presented here together.

An appropriate headline to the story of Kingston's keyboard industry would be "Pianos on Princess Street," because more than a dozen piano manufacturers and retailers over their period 1862 – 1939 were located at seven different addresses on this major municipal artery.[46] The focal point of the industry was the marvellous building located at the corner of Princess and Ontario streets.

In 1820 British architect George Browne was commissioned to design and erect a building capacious enough to accommodate the largest grocery business in Canada West. The four-storey structure, cut from limestone slabs in nearby quarries, still stands. For three-quarters of a century, the twang of tuned piano wires bounced off its stone walls.

About 1862 John C. Fox, a talented piano craftsman, arrived in Ontario from New York. In a small corner of the great stone building, Fox opened a modest pianoforte manufactory while his brother, Charles F. Fox, retailed the instruments from the storefront. (See Figures 89 and 90.) According to the Kingston city directories of the period, the Fox brothers were joined by George M. Weber in 1865, with Weber becoming the principal owner four years later following the death of John Fox.

A succession of smaller piano manufacturers flourished in Kingston during these decades. In 1873 Joseph Reyner manufactured instruments at 82 King St. That same year Charles Mee & Co. was active on Cove St. And in 1875 James Purdy made several pianos a month at 188 Princess St. The names F.C. Cline, John Breden, Jr. and John Rappe also appear as small-scale piano makers around 1878 – 80.[47]

By 1881 it appears that George Weber had moved part of his operation to 186 Wellington St. while his brother, John, and W.H. Stevenson had joined the firm and were carrying on the business at the main Princess St. location. Another person James McManus, was a short-term partner in 1885. (See Figure 91.)

Around 1887, the G.M. Weber Piano Company was renamed Stevenson & Co., but then reverted to Weber Piano Company as principal investors and strong personalities washed back and forth through the Kingston industry like the stormy waves on her Lake Ontario shore.

By 1893 seven retail outlets were marketing pianos in Kingston. Mason & Risch, W. Doherty, and

Figure 90. Ad from the Kingston City Directory, 1865.

Figure 89. Photo that accompanied an account concerning Wormwith Piano Co. as printed in the **Daily British Whig,** *July 1909. This building (still standing) is at the corner of Princess and Ontario streets.*

R.S. Williams all had stores here. And one enterprising firm, R. J. McDowall, boasted a regular supply of pianos from nine different companies and organs from ten.

The affairs of the Weber company continued to fluctuate. Kingston city directories show E.J.B. Pense as the proprietor in 1893, with W.H. Wormwith, Richard McMullan, George Lee, and Thomas Connor listed as company principals in 1896. McMullan-name pianos appeared for a short time, but the name that would dominate the company's next twenty years was William Wormwith.

Renamed the Wormwith Piano Co. about 1907, this main Kingston piano firm produced several thousand fine-quality instruments. An industrial-profile supplement to the Daily British Whig in 1909 described the company as giving

> "employment to a large staff of experienced workmen, and [the company] finds it more and more difficult to meet the demands of the trade. They have agencies in New Brunswick, Nova Scotia, Quebec, Manitoba, British Columbia and Ontario; and every piano they send out is an advertisement both for the company and for the city itself where such a concern is located. Although the trade is mostly confined to Canada, the company does business with all parts of the civilized globe and wherever the name Wormwith is seen the city of Kingston is known as the home of good pianos." (See Figure 92.)

Although the factory was partially destroyed by fire in 1908, Wormwith rebuilt his operation into a roaring success. Both Wormwith and Weber name lines appeared and several styles of Weber player pianos were constructed from 1912-15. By 1916, the aging Wormwith had brought in C.Y. Chown and H.W. Richardson as partners, although he remained president and general manager for the next two years. On Wormwith's retirement (by early 1919) Henry Richardson bought

Figure 91. Ad from the Kingston City Directory, 1883.

the controlling shares and incorporated the business with the old name Weber Piano Company Kingston Limited. At the time, 1,800 pianos a year were being turned out by seventy-five tradesmen. By 1920 those figures had increased to 2,000 units annually and over 100 workers. Still another partner, Henry Breathwaite, entered the company in 1929, assuming the role of president and general manager by 1935.

During this period, however, the Kingston piano industry was on the rocks. About 1928 a line of Weber pianos had been sold to the Heintzman company for its use as a secondary, inexpensive line. When the difficult mid-1930's arrived, and the demise of Weber was imminent, Heintzman contracted Sherlock-Manning in Clinton to manufacture the Weber line. The fallboard decal read "WEBER – Made for Heintzman by Sherlock-Manning." The Clinton company produced about 100 instruments a year under this arrangement. By 1939 the Weber Piano Company Ltd. had to declare bankruptcy. Lesage bought the remaining assets.

The stencil name "Columbia" was a line produced by Weber/Wormwith c. 1909 – 17.

Weber serial numbers
1875 – 7,000   1885 – 8,100   1900 – 13,000
1910 – 19,000 1915 – 26,200 1920 – 33,600
1925 – 39,000 1930 – 41,000

(Manufactured by Sherlock-Manning and Lesage)
1940 – 109,000 1945 – 112,000 1950 – 113,000
1955 – 117,00 1960 – 120,000

Wormwith serial numbers
1900 – 12,600 1905 – 15,100 1910 – 19,200
1914 – 26,000 1917 – 27,700

Figure 92. Ad from the Kingston City Directory, 1909.

Figure 93. Ad from the Kingston City Directory, 1919.

R.S. WILLIAMS & SONS

One of the most enduring music businesses (though not always a manufacturer) in Canadian history, the R.S. Williams company got its start in Hamilton, Ontario. Although some sources suggest that Richard Sugden Williams opened his own instrument-repair shop in 1849, and a 1917 ad implies the same, this date is a little premature since young Williams, born on 12 April 1834, was only fifteen years old at the time.

Serving several years of apprenticeship with William Townsend, a Hamilton melodeon maker, Williams appears to have been a willing student and quick learner. He opened a small shop in Toronto about 1854. While selling a few imported square pianos, his main trade was manufacturing mandolins, banjos, and later guitars, violins, and brass instruments.[48]

Close to twenty years elapsed before Williams realized that there were larger dollars to be made from the production of larger instruments. Acquiring an interest in the Canada Organ and Piano Company, Oshawa, around 1873, Williams finally took total control of the firm and moved his entire operation to Oshawa in 1888.

As *Historical Sketches of Oshawa*, a 1921 publication, states, in 1888 "Mr. Williams purchased the property of the Joseph Hall works and expended a large sum on money in adapting the works to his business. The old buildings were thoroughly repaired and re-roofed with slate, and new hard wood floors. Extensive new buildings were erected on Duke (later Richmond) Street, very much lengthening the front of the works, affording the necessary floor space."[49]

An active promoter of his firm, Williams had established retail outlets in Calgary, Winnipeg, London, and Montreal by 1903. The

Figure 94. Employees in the varnish and rubbing deck department at R.S. Williams, c. 1922.

Figure 95. A 1917 ad run by R.S. Williams.

Figure 96. The action-finishing department at R.S. Williams Company, 1914.

Figure 97. A special addition to the west end of R.S. Williams's Oshawa factory, the organ department was a bustling aspect of the firm's business. This 1910 photo highlights the fact that all pipe organs were assembled and tested in the factory, and then shipped and installed in the church or public building that had commissioned the work.

expansion continued after his death on 24 February 1906, as son Robert moved the family business to the international market-place. By 1920 a popular player piano had been developed and a huge export trade with Australia and New Zealand was well in place.50

When Robert's brother, Richard Sugden Williams, Jr. entered the company about 1909, the firm became known as R.S. Williams & Sons Ltd. All departments were expanded at the Oshawa factory during the 1910 – 20 period, and by 1921 the weekly payroll for the company's 275 employees amounted to $6,000.

A later co-owner and president, Frederick W. Bull, witnessed the darker days of the Williams business from the mid-1920s onward. By 1932 the factory was shut down, although a retail trade of imported string and brass instruments continued in Toronto until the early 1950s.

The lines made and/or distributed by Williams were: Beethoven – bought from J.W. Shaw about 1908; Canada; Ennis – from 1911; Everson – originally a US piano; Krydner; New Scale Williams; Plaola – possibly a name taken over by Williams and used on a player-piano line; Princess; Schubert; Williams.

A wonderful collection of eighteen photographs depicting various aspects of the Williams business c. 1910 – 22 is owned by The Robert McLaughlin Gallery, Oshawa. Four appear in this account. The Royal Ontario Museum, Toronto, owns a fine collection of instruments originally assembled, and later donated to the museum, by Robert Williams.

Williams serial numbers*

1890 – 11,000	1893 – 14,000	1896 – 16,000
1899 – 18,000	1901-19,000	1903 – 20,000
1904 – 21,000	1908 – 23,000	1911 – 27,000
1912 – 29,000	1915 – 34,000	1917 – 40,000
1919 – 44,000	1922 – 56,000	1925 – 62,000
1928 – 70,000	1930 – 73,000	

*As the various lines were introduced, one consecutive set of serial numbers seems to have been applied.

Figure 98. Ad from the Farmer's Advocate and Home Magazine, *October 1911, p.1623.*

WILLIS & COMPANY

In 1869 Alexander Willis was a restless young school teacher turned divinity student turned money trader. That summer, wanting to do more with his life than teach, preach, or make money, he packed his grip, said goodbye to his Nova Scotian home, and walked to Montreal. After spending a couple of months in the employ of a bookseller, and another few weeks with a picture dealer, young Willis finally came to a vocational decision. He wanted to be a businessman.

An opportunity to become the Maritime representative for a large Quebec sewing-machine manufacturer presented itself. Willis grabbed it, moved back to Nova Scotia, and opened a successful retail outlet in Stellarton. But as business through Atlantic Canada was sewn up, wanderlust struck again. By 1875 Willis was back in Montreal complete with a new name. A romantic at heart, he had always admired the works of American poet Nathaniel Parker Willis (no relation) and thought that the addition of "Parker" to his own name gave it a certain ring. From that time until his death in 1934, Alexander Parker Willis was known affectionately to his family, employees, and business contacts as "A.P."

By 1884 enterprising Willis had dropped his sewing-machine line and begun pushing a more popular household appliance – the piano. Carrying R.S. Williams and Bell pianos and American instruments made by Chickering, Emerson (Boston), and Knabe (Baltimore), his firm prospered as a principal Montreal music outlet. Located in a three-storey building at 1824 Notre Dame St., the Willis company quickly learned the value of advertising and customer relations. Prolific in the distribution of coloured lithographed trade cards and scented (ink) blotting papers, the firm also presented a brocaded silk scarf to each piano purchaser and an elaborate music-instruction book to each organ buyer.

When Willis obtained the distribution rights for the Knabe piano, he employed another advertising strategy. In New York the Steinway Company had long promoted its product by inviting world-class singers to present concerts in which a Steinway grand was used for accompaniment. Willis thought that it was a great idea and proceeded to bring internationally acclaimed vocalists and pianists to Montreal, where they performed at concerts graced by the presence of high-quality Knabe pianos. Over a period of three decades, Montrealers were treated to the talents of some of the greatest classical artists of the day. As a result of these promotions, A.P. Willis not only pleased the music loving public but sold thousands of pianos.

Old "A.P." was a clever businessman. If the terms of the installment payments for an instrument were too steep for a family to make, he would barter a piano for other goods and services. One of his sons (John James Willis, from whose unpublished family history most of this information was gleaned), recalls grocers, shoemakers, tailors, and other tradesmen often coming to the Willis home to deliver items of trade. And J.J. Willis remembered that during the smallpox epidemic of 1885, he sat bare-armed in the parlour while one Dr. McConnell administered vaccinations to the family in return for a piano payment.

In February 1887 "A.P."'s brother, Robert, came to Montreal following the failure of his dry-

Figure 99. Ad from the Canadian Music Journal, vol. 2 (Winter 1957).

goods business in Stellarton. His entry into the Willis operation was eagerly anticipated because of his personable manner and abilities as a salesman. A bout with consumption, however, prevented him from making a long-lasting contribution to the business. He was dead within two years. (Robert Willis was grandfather to Austin and Frank Willis of CBC radio and television fame).

By 1907 "A.P." had grown discontented with the sale of pianos made by others. He bought the controlling interests of Demase Lesage's piano business in Ste-Thérèse-de-Blainville and soon had a wide variety of his own "name" pianos rolling off the production line. (See also Lesage.) Before long, 2,000 instruments a year were being made.[51] Employment at the factory would peak at 150 workers turning out close to 3,000 pianos annually in later years.

Albert Willis, ("A.P." 's son) joined the business in 1911, remaining in the trade for the next fifty-eight years. His brothers Robert, William, and Inglis also spent time in the company. The family firm did well during the 1920s and even through the difficult 1930s, a decade that claimed all but a handful of Canadian piano companies. In 1938 a third generation of Willis men entered the business. Matt Willis (son of John James Willis) would likewise spend much of his working life in the piano trade. Following the Second World War he was appointed sales manager and company trouble-shooter. Spending up to six months a year "on the road," Matt covered Canada from coast to coast as well as the New England states.

As much of the demand for pianos fell off

Figure 100. A Willis ad as it appeared in the Canadian Music Journal, *vol. 2 (Spring 1958).*

during the 1940s and 1950s the Willis organization diversified. Manufacturing a high-class line of furniture (trade-named Spencer-Wood), the company also produced wooden radio and TV cabinets for Fleetwood, Clairtone, Phillips, Marconi, Dumont, and Northern Electric, and cases for Hammond and Lowrey organs. With branches in Halifax, Moncton, Quebec, Trois-Rivières, and Ottawa, the Willis piano was kept available to potential customers all across eastern Canada.

Willis manufactured and distributed a wide variety of instruments over the years. Its own "name" pianos were produced in about seven upright styles, four grands (from 4'8" to 6'6") and three design choices for a 36" high drop-action piano. The latter, while initially selling well, was never fully accepted by piano retailers. Matt Willis contends that the 36" piano *should* have been promoted. As he argues, "When the kids have had their fill with lessons after a couple of years, you don't want a clumsy, big ornament stuck in the living room forever. At least with the 36" piano you can put family pictures and flowers and things on it, still play it if you want to, and have it blend in reasonably well with the height of couches, chairs and other furniture in the room." A good point, but apparently the Canadian trade remained unconvinced.

After a century of bringing music and happiness to the homes of countless thousands, the Willis company closed the doors on 17 October 1978. A fire consumed its old factory buildings in Ste-Thérèse-de-Blainville on the morning of 17 June 1981.

Willis serial number

1905 – 2,000	1910 – 6,000	1915 – 12,000	1935 – 34,500	1940 – 36,500	1945 – 38,500
1920 – 22,000	1925 – 28,500	1930 – 34,000	1950 – 42,000	1955 – 44,000	1960 – 45,500
			1965 – 47,000 ♪		

Figure 101. Matthew Willis poses in March 1989 beside a piano made by his company.

CHAPTER SEVEN

The Pianos Of Canada: A To Z

The following alphabetical list enumerates all known brand- and stencil-name pianos manufactured in Canada, as well as all individuals and companies known to have been involved as manufacturers of Canadian pianos. In some instances little, if any, information has survived. In other cases considerable documentary materials, photographs, illustrations, and old ads provide well-rounded profiles of individual companies and product lines. Apart from Canadian-made pianos, imported brands that were distributed by Canadian firms have been included if it appears that some of the final manufacturing or assembly was done in this country. Scores of other foreign brand- and stencil-name pianos from the United States, Britain, Germany, France, Italy, Japan, and Korea have been sold by retailers in Canada, but such "finished product" items are not included in this listing.

The names appearing in italics have been documented in detail in chapter six. Cross references, where applicable, appear at the end of each account. While every effort has been made to document this material accurately and fairly, I want to offer my apologies for any errors and/or omissions

ACADEMY – made by *SHERLOCK-MANNING*. This 45"-high piano was built to withstand rugged use and constant moving. Thousands were sold to school boards across Canada during the 1960s and 1970s.

ALEXANDRA – Misspelled as "Alexander" by the two leading North American piano atlases, the Alexandra, made by *WILLIS PIANO COMPANY*, was named after the wife of King Edward VII (reigned 1901–10). A photo on hand at the Bowmanville (Ontario) Museum shows members of the Canadian Manufacturers' Association posing on the lawn of Windsor Castle after being presented to Edward VII and Queen Alexandra in 1905. J.W. Alexander, president of the *DOMINION ORGAN & PIANO COMPANY*, was in this delegation, as, no doubt, were representatives of several other Canadian piano firms. The Willis company, however, was the first to capitalize on the use of the regal name. This model was in production c. 1906–15. [1] (See also *WILLIS*)

AMHERST PIANOS – The heyday of the piano had been very good to the McDonald Piano and Music Company, the largest piano retailer in

Maritime Canada in 1910. J.A. McDonald had every reason to smile as he built branch after branch in major centres all across Nova Scotia and New Brunswick. But by 1912 his annual sales were outstripping the capacity of the major piano factory with which he had been dealing. "Why don"t we open one up here, boys!" must have been his wide-eyed call as he proposed a piano factory for his hometown of Amherst. Within days enough businessmen and investors had jumped on his band-wagon and $500,000 capital had been secured.

Hiring many of the top designers and personnel from the dying Blundall Piano Company, Toronto, and buying up the existing small company of H.A. Hillcoat Pianos, Amherst, the new firm Amherst Pianos Ltd. had production well underway by early 1913.

Almost immediately the company began capitalizing on the player-piano craze. A well made, but pricey item, its $750 player was offered as first prize in 1913 to the person who sold the most subscriptions to the *Busy East* magazine. Soon, the aggressive firm had built up a network of 200 retail dealers from Quebec City to Vancouver, and was even exporting its uprights to Europe. Following the great explosion of 16 December 1917 in Halifax harbour, a "scratch and dent" sale was held in Amherst. With an ad that was circulated far and wide, the company promised to sell this lot of pianos on terms of $2 down and $1 a week, adding that "no matter where you live, come here to this sale. We will pay freight on any piano. We will pay your railway fare to and from the sale. We will give you a stool. We will give you an iron clad guarantee."[2] Who could refuse?

By 1925 or so slick campaigns and give-aways weren't enough to keep the company afloat. Nor was diversification into organ repair and even gramophone production. Rising freight rates and increasing competition from other forms of entertainment caused Amherst Pianos Ltd. to close its doors in 1928. A small group of Amherst workers picked up some of the company equipment, actions, and piano parts, and formed the Cumberland Piano Company. This firm possibly operated in a small way in Amherst (and later Toronto), but there is no record of it past 1930.[3]

GEORGE ANDERSON – one of the first piano makers in Nova Scotia. Anderson had been employed in the firm of Brockley & Co., Halifax, as early as 1856. By 1863 John Misner had entered the business with Brockley and Anderson, the company name being changed to Brockley & Misner. Misner left shortly after that time and by 1867 George Anderson had been admitted as a full partner. The firm was one of Canada's first active piano exporters.[4] (See also Brockley & Co.)

ED ARCHAMBAULT – Established in Montreal in 1896, the Archambault company was to become synonymous with Montreal music. A publisher of Canadian composers and instruction materials, and dealing in Bell, Thomas, Pratte, and Lesage pianos, the Archambault retail outlet was truly a landmark on the Quebec music scene. About 1915 the Archambault piano appeared. With the exception of the sounding board, which was a US import, the instrument was totally manufactured in Montreal. It survived until 1924, when the line was taken over by *WEBER* in Kingston. The remainder of the retail business flourished until the 1970s.[5]

THE AUTONOLA – a name used in 1906 by *BELL* for their first player-piano model.

BAGNALL ORGAN & PIANO COMPANY – John Bagnall, a pianoforte tuner and repairman, had started in the trade in 1849. Moving to Victoria, British Columbia, about 1862, he began manufacturing several reed organs a month, with square pianos added to his line by 1871. During an apparent lapse in manufacturing from 1872–81, Bagnall operated a retail shop on

Government St, distributing, among other things, the German "Newmeyer Quadruplex Piano" and the French "Bord-Favorite Piano."6 By 1881, however, the *British Colonist* reported that "the high Canadian tariff has been found to press heavily upon the importation, and Bagnall and Co., after examining thoroughly into the matter, have decided to proceed to the manufacture of organs ... and pianos as well. Several instruments are now underweigh [sic], and in a short time the public will be gratified by listening to the sweet tones of the first homemade organ. The firm desire every encouragement. They throw into the work energy, practical knowledge and capital. With these desiderata in hand, success is certain to attend their enterprise."7 The firm was taken over by Charles Goodwin & Company about 1886.

BARCLAY, GLASS & COMPANY – Dundas, Ontario. Period unknown.

BARTHELMES – Brothers Franz Ludwig and Alexander August Barthelmes were prolific inventors. The Canadian Patent Office has seven or more of their well-illustrated piano inventions, which range from elaborate action modifications to several unique sounding-board and iron-plate designs. And while no record of a piano or individual company bears their name, they are worthy of mention as notable contributors to the industry over the period 1889–1904. They were perhaps principals of or associates with one of the many Toronto manufacturers of the period and went on to become a major supplier of piano actions and parts to other Canadian companies.8

BEETHOVEN – A stencil-name piano made by George Ducharme, Montreal, 1891–98. By 1905 the line was produced by J.W. Shaw (Montreal) and later by *R.S. WILLIAMS*.

BELL PIANO & ORGAN COMPANY (See Chapter Six)

BELLOLIAN – a name used by *BELL* in 1902 for its first piano-player model.

BELMONT – originally a name used by *BELL* until that firm was bought out by *LESAGE* which used the name from 1934 onward.

BERLIN PIANO & ORGAN COMPANY – In June 1890, a consortium of six men formed the Berlin Piano & Organ Company. The city council of Berlin (Kitchener after 1916) passed a bylaw that year providing a $10,000 incentive grant over a ten-year period on condition that the new firm would employ forty to sixty workers. The principals were J.M. Staebler, Frederick Snyder, E.P. Clement, Jacob Kauffman, F.G. Gardiner, and John Fennell. All apparently were local businessmen who felt that their small city and neighbouring Waterloo could support a piano and organ industry. But just to make sure, they recruited several skilled tradesmen who had extensive experience in the piano business. One was E. Birch, who previously had spent seventeen years with assorted Canadian and American manufacturers. It was at his insistence that a totally new sound-board design and a third (or practice) pedal were introduced to the Berlin piano lines. The latter was proclaimed as "an ingenious device by means of which students play softly and the tonal mechanism of the instrument is protected from pounding."9 (What a selling feature for parents of a would-be prodigy!)

The product was hailed locally as a wonderful invention and a somewhat less than objective editorial in the *Berlin News Record* of 14 April 1900 sweetly stated that "as a result of the new improvements, the Berlin piano has a smoothness, purity and brilliancy of tone and perfection of action and touch that must captivate the musical public." While not pursuing the export market to the same extent that most of their contemporaries were doing, the Berlin Piano & Organ Company appears to have sold at least some instruments

Berlin Pianos and Organs

SOLD ON EASY TERMS OF PAYMENT

WARRANTED FOR FIVE YEARS

Over Four Hundred Instruments sold in Waterloo County during the past Three years.

Visitors to Berlin are welcome to our Warerooms, 25 King Str.

SOLD ONLY BY

F. G. GARDINER,
Secretary Berlin Piano & Organ Co. L't'd

Figure 102. Ad from 11 October 1894.

outside the Berlin-Waterloo area. A dozen or more requests about these products have been received at the Kitchener Public Library. They span the past thirty years and a 2,000 mile radius.

Sometime between 1896 and 1905, W.H. Snyder & Co. purchased the firm and its trade name began to appear on several piano and organ lines, the Berlin piano line being retained as well. Then in 1906 the large New York piano conglomerate Foster-Armstrong Co. bought out the operation. The Berlin and Snyder names were dropped and the popular US piano names of Haines Bros. and Marshall & Wendell appeared along with the Foster-Armstrong line.

A slow death, however, set in for the new company from the First World War onward. By 1924 business had all but dried up. SHERLOCK-MANNING bought the remaining assets and the Foster-Armstrong, Haines Bros., and Marshall & Wendell lines contined to appear for several years under its banner.[10]

BERNHARDT – a small retail operation in Windsor, Ontario, that assembled and distributed Miessner electronic pianos, c. 1957.

BESSEMER – a name used by NEWCOMBE.

A.R. BLACKBURN & SONS – Toronto, c. 1912. Possibly a retailer only. No other information located.

ROBERT BLOUIN PIANOS – Sherbrooke, Quebec, 1949–74.

BLUNDALL PIANO COMPANY – Toronto, 1900–13. Factory located at 13 McKenzie St with a retail shop at 144 Spadina Ave in 1912.

WILLIAM BOHRER – Montreal, 1883–1901. With partner Theobald Messmer, Bohrer filed several interesting piano patents over the period 1884–99. A system of "portable, auxilliary pedals" and a transposing device that could be attached to any piano seem to have been hallmark of their inventiveness. The Bohrer piano was apparently manufactured under unknown names by contemporaries in the Montreal trade.[11]

BOWLES – Quebec City, c. 1850.

THOMAS BOYD – Uxbridge, Ontario, c. 1891. Although the *Encyclopedia of Music in Canada* lists Boyd as a manufacturer, no record of a piano bearing his name could be found. He may have been in partnership with one Charles Wassan Small (Uxbridge, 1891), who later filed several piano patents from Toronto about 1909. The small town of Uxbridge was also the home of the Uxbridge Piano Company and the Palmer Piano Company.

Figure 103. A classified ad printed in the Globe, 10 August 1912.

Boyd and Small were no doubt associated with one of these firms. A short-lived piano business called Small & McArthur also found a home in Uxbridge in 1898.

BRANTFORD PIANO COMPANY – Brantford, Ontario, c. 1890. *MORRIS, FEILD & ROGERS* of Listowel, Ontario, took over the assets in 1892.

BROCKLEY & MISNER PIANOFORTES – About 1795 Thomas Brockley packed his duffel bag and walked out of Scotland *en route* to London. His dream was to obtain a position with the famous Shudi & Broadwood (later Broadwood & Sons) pianoforte company.

The dream realized, Brockley worked diligently with Broadwood and German craftsman W.W. Stodart (patriarch of the later great line of New York piano builders named Stodart). By 1820 Brockley had induced his eldest son, twenty-four-year-old Thomas, Jr, into the trade.

Following the death of the senior Brockley in 1826, young Thomas was elevated to a foreman's position at Broadwood's, remaining there for another thirty years. But in 1856 the lure of the stories about the streets paved with gold in "New Scotland," were too much for him. Setting sail from Britain, he arrived in Halifax and shortly after set up shop with J. Phillips, one of Canada's pioneer piano makers. A year later Brockley's son, Alfred W., arrived in Nova Scotia and, together with John Misener and George Anderson, established one of the finest keyboard instrument companies in the land.

Brockley designs were classic. A Halifax newspaper reported that a beautiful "seven octave piano with Italian walnut woodwork" was proudly purchased from the firm in 1870 by Dr W.N. Wickwire for $360.[12]

By 1872 business was booming. The firm moved from the corner of Duke and Barrington streets to 107 Granville St, putting the factory in the upper two storeys and a retail shop in the storefront.

A city directory for 1876 indicated that "they manufacture Pianos of all styles, ranging in price from $200 to $1,000, consisting of Cottage or upright Pianos, which on account of their compactness and other advantages are becoming the prevailing style everywhere – also square and grand Pianos. The best materials are used in their construction and they are peculiarly adapted by their strength and the quality of materials, for transportation and use in any climate."13

Brockley pianos won top awards at many trade shows of their day, including a £25 award for their cottage (upright) model at the London International Exhibition of 1862. As an export item, Brockley instruments were found as far west as Manitoba in 1875 as well as in the United States, the West Indies, and even England. The firm does not appear to have survived past the mid-1890s.

GEORGE BROWN, JOHN MUNRO & COMPANY – Montreal, c. 1860. Originally a Boston piano company. Extent of Canadian distribution unknown.

CAMEO – a name used by *MASON & RISCH*.

THE CANADA – a stencil name used by *R.S. WILLIAMS*.

CANADA ORGAN & PIANO COMPANY – Oshawa, Ontario, 1873–1902. The small firm was absorbed into *R.S. WILLIAMS* in 1902.

CANADIAN PIANO COMPANY – established by Thomas F.G. Foisy in Ste-Thérèse-de-Blainville, Quebec, 1888–91. *LESAGE* bought the business in March of 1891 and carried its line for many years. C.W. Lindsay and *WILLIS* (both Montreal) – and later *MASON & RISCH* – carried the line for short periods.

CARLTON – a name used by *WILLIS*.

CECILIAN PIANO COMPANY – Toronto, 1904–22. An apparent manufacturer of player pianos only, this company had its product sold and distributed by *HEINTZMAN* from 1906. The company was bought out by Stanley Pianos in 1922.

LOUIS CHARBONNEAU – Montreal, c. 1889.

CHARLES PIANO COMPANY – New Westminister, British Columbia, c. 1920.

CHOPIN – a name used by *MASON & RISCH*.

CLASSIC – a name used by *MASON & RISCH* 1909–25. Serial # 15,000 in 1919 jumped to series 93,000 by 1925. This is a classic example of how piano serial numbers could seemingly indicate large volume sales. A more accurate estimate of the number of these instruments sold during this period would be closer to 500 per year or less.

V.W. CLAUDE & COMPANY – Montreal, c. 1898.

CLAYTON – imported from Michigan and partially assembled by Grinnell Bros., Windsor, Ontario. Limited numbers were distributed in southern Ontario from 1910 to 1940.

F.C. CLINE – Kingston, Ontario, c. 1868. (See also *WEBER/WORMWITH*.)

CLINTON – a name used by *DOHERTY PIANO & ORGAN COMPANY* about 1913. The name was later used briefly by *SHERLOCK-MANNING*.

COLONIAL PIANO COMPANY – Ste.Thérèse-de-Blainville, Quebec, 1915–27. Distributed the Saint-Saens piano provincially.

COLUMBIA – a name used by *WEBER*. Five digit serial numbers:
1909 – 27,000   1910 – 28,000   1911 – 29,000
1912 – 30,000   1913 – 31,000   1914 – 32,000
1915 – 34,000   1916 – 36,000   1917 – 37,000

CONCERTO – a model name (not stencilled on the instrument) used by *LESAGE*, c. 1978–86.

CONCORD CANADIAN – by *LESAGE* (as above).

CONTINENTAL EURO – by *LESAGE* (as above).

CONSOLIDATED – a name used by Crossin & Martens Piano Manufacturing Company, Toronto, c. 1904–08.

CRAIG PIANO COMPANY – Montreal, 1856–1930. Located at 1190 de Montigny, the firm had been previously known as Labelle & Craig (1854–56), David Craig, proprietor. The Craig line was absorbed by *LESAGE* in 1930. Serial numbers from 1913 to 1919 range from 23,000 – 29,000, a good example of how number series were often chosen to correspond to year numbers. (That is, the second digit of the serial number would correspond to the fourth digit of the year. And even if only 300 pianos were produced and numbered, the serial numbers for the next year would jump by 1,000. This method can be systematically observed for many piano manufacturers although numerous exceptions occur.)

E. CROSS & COMPANY – Toronto, c. 1898.

CROSSIN & MCPHILLIPS – In 1879 this small piano operation began business in a narrow shop at 71 Dundas St, London, Ontario. William McPhillips and Crossin were no doubt craftsmen who had learned the piano trade in a larger business and decided to venture out on their own. They turned out several instruments a month which, along with other "name" square pianos, were sold in their retail shop. But before their first anniversary a fire gutted the operation and manufacturing ceased. Several years later McPhillips reorganized, moved a couple of blocks east, and began a lucrative musical-instrument trade. Later, as a dealer for Gerhard Heintzman, McPhillips offered pianos to Londoners until 1922. Crossin had moved to Toronto after the fire and set up business with a new partner. [14] (See next entry.)

CROSSIN & MARTENS PIANO MANUFAC-

TURING COMPANY – Toronto, 1883–1908. Made the Consolidated piano line.

CUMBERLAND PIANO COMPANY – Amherst, Nova Scotia. Formed out of the failing Amherst Piano Company, the 1928 venture made a move to Toronto about 1930 but lasted only a couple of years. (See also Amherst Pianos Ltd.)

DARLEY & ROBINSON – Oshawa, Ontario, 1870. Became Oshawa Organ & Melodeon Mfg. Co. in 1871. On its move to Bowmanville, Ontario, in 1875, the company was renamed *DOMINION ORGAN & PIANO COMPANY*.

DAVID & MICHAUD – Montreal, 1917–23. Brothers Euclide and Jeremie David and Oswald Michaud were principals of this small company. While the Davids did not remain in the business long, Michaud went on to greater things. (See also entry for Oswald Michaud.)

DENHOLM – a name used by *WILLIS*, c. 1919.

WILLIAM DENNIS – Montreal, c. 1834–53. Dennis was later a partner with J.W. Herbert & Co.

DERBY – a name used by Stanley, c. 1896.

DIPLOMA – a name used by *BELL PIANO & ORGAN COMPANY* for its melodeons in 1864, and then later (c. 1900) for a line of upright pianos.

W. DOHERTY & COMPANY (see Chapter Six)

DOMINION – a name used briefly by Rainer & Company, Whitby, Ontario, c. 1866. (No connection with the *DOMINION ORGAN & PIANO COMPANY*)

DOMINION ORGAN & PIANO COMPANY (see Chapter Six)

DRAPER BROS. & REID LTD. – Clinton, Ontario. (See *SHERLOCK-MANNING*.)

DREHER – possibly associated with the name Steinbach. *MASON & RISCH* distributed a Steinbach & Dreher line from 1904–1911.

GEORGE DUCHARME – Montreal, 1891–98. (See also Beethoven.)

NOAH DURANT – Vankleek Hill, Ontario, c. 1908.

EATON'S – The largest department-store chain in Canada offered pianos regularly from 1900 onward. With its volume buying power it was able – as with so many other items – to demand a piano with its own stencil name. The pianos were generally of fair quality and usually manufactured for them by one of the larger Toronto manufacturers. Eaton's 1909 catalogue offered a choice between a "Colonial" or "Louis XIV" model priced at $185. [15]

EDMUND PIANO COMPANY – New Westminister, British Columbia, 1924– c. 1950, Edmund C. Charles, proprietor. The company factory at 715 Carnavon St was complemented by retail space at 415 Columbia St. [16]

ENNIS PIANO COMPANY – Originally Ennis & Ennis, this company had its roots in Hamilton, Ontario, going back to 1863. Producing a moderately fine instrument at competitive prices, the Ennis product sold well until the early days of 1903. From that time onward, lack of aggressive sales activity and a highly competitive market caused production to slump. On the morning of

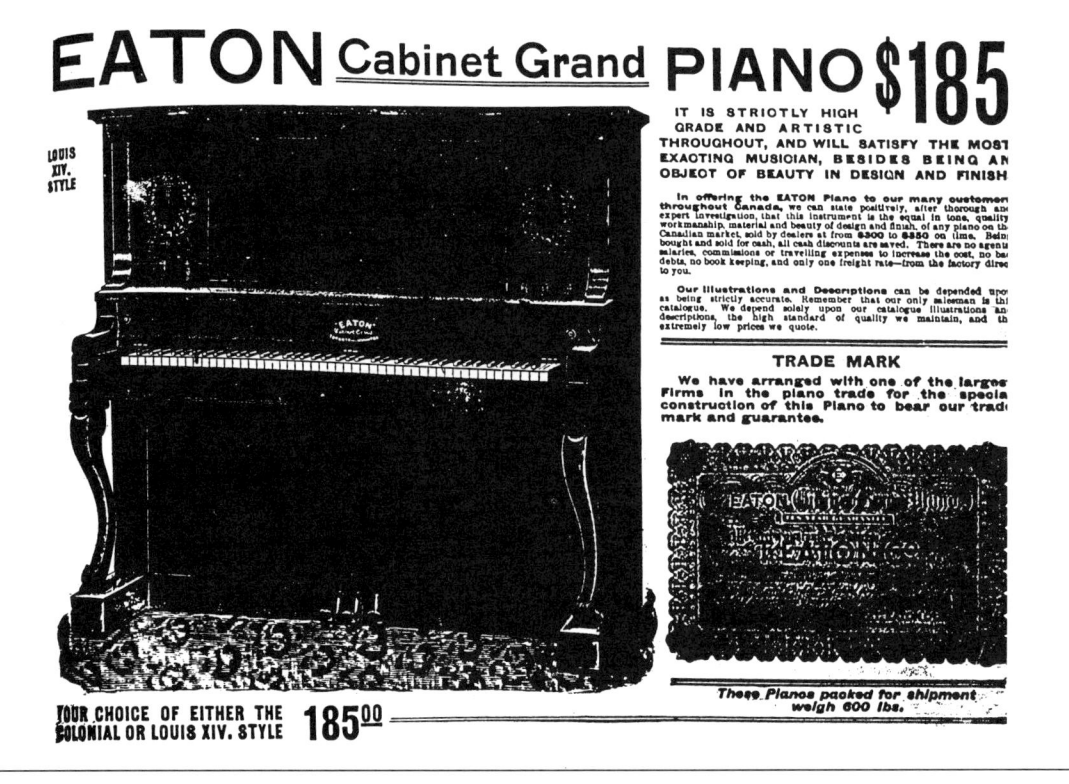

Figure 104. Illustration from Eaton's fall and winter catalogue, 1909-10, p. 151.

> **Piano Manufacturers**
>
> NEW WESTMINSTER
>
> **EDMUND PIANO CO.**
> Edmund C. Charles, Proprietor
> Maker of the "EDMUND" PIANO
> Phone 2236
>
> Factory: Show Room:
> 715 Carnarvon St.   415 Columbia St.

Figure 105. Listing from the Greater Vancouver City Directory For 1938, p. 1905.

17 August 1905 calamity struck the Ennis plant. A neighbour close to the site at 164 King St on looking out his bedroom window, saw the whole building engulfed in flames. Although the estimated loss on the building and its contents was calculated at just over $21,000, the untimely fire was too much for the company to bear.

The next morning, as he toured the scene, Mr. Ennis was quoted by a local reporter: "Everything is practically destroyed. We employ about thirty men, but the factory has been shut down since July on account of business being slack. It was just starting to pick up again, though, and we intended starting our works shortly."

As the intrepid reporter nosed around the area, he encountered an Ennis employee named Horning who claimed that he had seen small boys smoking cigarettes in the yard next to the factory. "One of the boys must have thrown a match or a cigarette into the basement, and that started the fire," Horning said.

"Do you think anyone would set the place on fire for spite," Ennis was asked.

"I don't know, and if I did it would not do for me to think out loud," he answered with a smile.

On this basis the local press printed the headline "Incendiary Fire at Ennis Piano Factory." An arsonist was apparently never apprehended although the Hamilton fire chief was later quoted as saying that "it looks as though someone was determined to burn the place down." [17]

Ennis rebuilt a portion of his operation, but things were never the same. By 1911 the limping firm couldn't keep up and the assets were auctioned. *R.S. WILLIAMS* controlled the rights to the Ennis name until the early 1930s, when *MASON & RISCH* acquired the line. Serial numbers from the time of the Williams takeover are:

1912 – 32,000   1917 – 42,000   1918 – 50,000
1920 – 53,000   1921 – 56,000   1925 – 66,000
1927 – 69,000   1929 – 75,000

EVANS BROS. PIANO COMPANY (see Chapter Six)

EVERSON – a name used by *R.S. WILLIAMS*. (Originally a US import piano.)

FARWELL PIANO COMPANY – a subsidiary of *DOMINION ORGAN AND PIANO COMPANY*, Bowmanville, Ontario. The Farwell piano line was named after the company president, J.H. Farwell (1878–94). An 1891 Farwell piano converted to a nickelodeon is part of a private collection in London, Ontario. The line was dropped by Dominion about 1910.

FEATHERSTON PIANO COMPANY – Montreal, 1893–99.

THOMAS F.G. FOISY – see Canadian Piano Company and also *LESAGE*.

FOSTER-ARMSTRONG COMPANY – One of several dozen companies consolidated under the banner of the huge Aeolian-American Corporation (formerly American Piano Company) in 1906. Haines Brothers and Marshall & Wendell brands were made by a Foster-Armstrong Canadian branch after its takeover of the Berlin Piano & Organ Company in Berlin (Kitchener) in 1906. The firm was absorbed by *SHERLOCK-MANNING* in 1924. (See also Berlin Piano & Organ Company.)

J.C. FOX – Kingston, Ontario (see *WEBER/WORMWITH*)

W. FRASER & SONS – Halifax, 1856–90. Fraser took over a portion of the earlier Halifax business of H. & J. Phillips (1845–59). (See also Williams & Leverman Piano Forte Manufactory.)

GATES ORGAN & PIANO COMPANY – Malvern Square, Nova Scotia, c. 1872–85. The company was later located in Truro.

GERHARD – a name used 1955-57 by Quidoz Pianos, Ste Thérèse-de-Blainville, Quebec. It was a

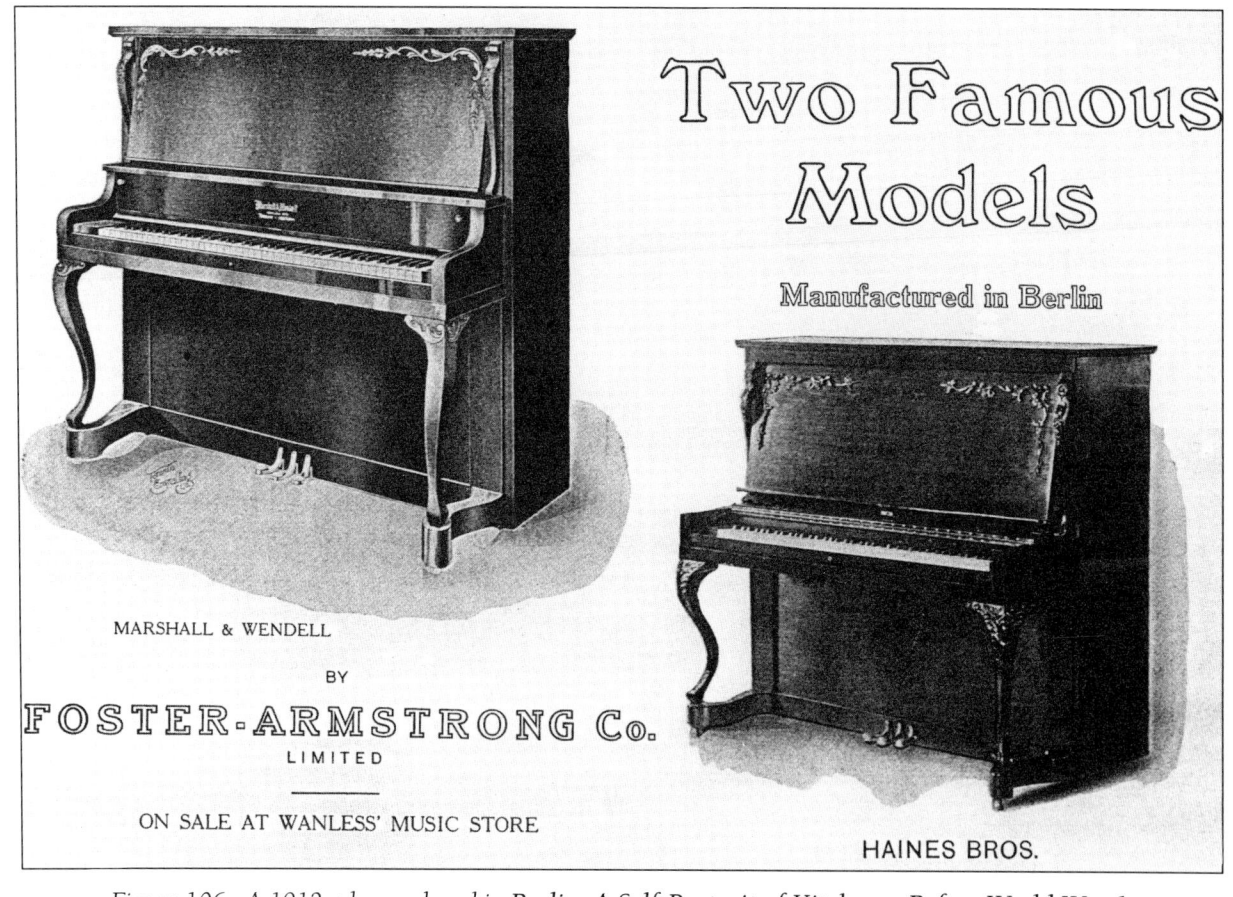

Figure 106. A 1912 ad reproduced in Berlin: A Self-Portrait of Kitchener Before World War 1, *(City of Kitchener, 1946) p.18.*

Figure 107. Ad from Roger's Photographic Advertising Album, Halifax, 1871.

Figure 108. W. Fraser & Sons Pianoforte shop, Halifax, 1871.

shortened name originally standing for Gerhard Heintzman for which the company had acquired some distribution rights.

CHARLES GOODWIN & COMPANY – manufacturer of the first grand pianos made and sold in British Columbia. The company, established in 1885 in Victoria, acquired the assets and tradesmen of the defunct Bagnall Organ & Piano Company in 1886. By 1890 the Victoria *British Colonist* reported that in the bustling factory "there are twenty-five (grand pianos) either finished or in the course of construction, and as many more have been sold and distributed about the province, giving entire satisfaction to their purchasers, who have signified the same by written testimony. A call at the factory will convince intending buyers not only that a first-class piano can be made at home, but also obtained for much less than its imported equal." [18] And while a further story in the same paper described a five-foot-long baby grand made from double-veneered rosewood as having "surprising volume of tone and singing capacity," the Goodwin company fell victim to bad days. By 1891 manufacturing had ceased. [19]

GOURLAY-ANGELUS – a line of player pianos manufactured by Gourlay, Winter & Leeming, c. 1915.

GOURLAY, WINTER & LEEMING – With its large retail outlet located at 188 Yonge St, Toronto, this company was a distributor for at least a dozen other Canadian, English, and American pianos. It was established in 1890 by Robert S. Gourlay, formerly general manager of *MASON & RISCH*. Partners Francis W. Winter and Thomas Leeming made up the business trio.[20]

The company did not begin manufacturing its own line of pianos until 1904, but within seven years its factory employed 225 people and by 1915 it claimed to have made over 8,000 instruments. With branches in several Ontario cities (including one at 114 Christina St, Sarnia) Gourlay, Winter & Leeming advertised far and wide. Its brochure *One Thousand Facts About*

Figure 109. Ad from the Farmer's Advocate and Home Magazine, *30 June 1904.*

Canada and its Art Pianos, written by employee Frank Yeigh, was mailed to homes from coast to coast.[21]

When Winter and Leeming retired during the First World War, Gourlay's sons David and Albert entered the business. Bankruptcy, however, broke the company in late 1923. SHERLOCK-MANNING picked up the remaining stock in the spring of 1924 and continued to offer the Gourlay-name piano from 1925–61.

Gourlay, Winter & Leeming serial numbers
1905 – 900   1909 – 1,800   1912 – 6,000
1915 – 8,500   1918 – 9,000   1923 – 16,000

GREENE – Toronto, c. 1910–24.

GRINNELL BROS. LTD. – Established as an organ manufacturer in Detroit in 1882, Grinnell Bros. did not enter the lucrative piano business until 1902. As a border city, neighbouring Windsor was often the specific target of the Detroit enterprise. But by September of 1908 Grinnell had opened a small branch factory in Windsor. Employing just four men in those early days, the firm seemed content to be a supplier of instruments to the Detroit-Windsor area only, not venturing much more than 100 miles from either city. With a retail outlet in neighbouring Sarnia and Chatham, Ontario, the Grinnell stores also acted as distributors for Nordheimer, Ennis, and R.S. Williams pianos, and during the 1920s carried at least seven brands of Canadian-made radios as well as victrolas, player-piano rolls, and sheet music.

A company motto that "music in the home makes it brighter and happier" was expanded upon in a 1927 *Border Cities Star* article commemorating the twenty-fifth anniversary of the Windsor arm of Grinnell Bros. It concluded that regular bursts of music in the home "result in a happier family, a happier citizen, a happier community and a happier nation. Grinnell Bros. has given hundreds of Border homes the music that has made them places of happiness and contentment."

Figure 110. Ad from The Walkerville News, *October 1928. While the Windsor branch had not been established until 1908, the twenty-fifth annual sales figure refers to the Detroit parent factory. Prior to establishing a manufacturing plant in Windsor, Grinnell had marketed Michigan-made products on the Ontario side of the St. Clair River.*

By 1927 twenty-five people were employed at the Windsor factory. And with the seriously polite yet ever-present rivalry between Windsor and Detroit always a factor in industry matters, the local press proudly boasted that all these employees were Canadian citizens. "Many of them own their own homes in this district ... and it is interesting to note that ten members of the headquarters' staff in Detroit are Canadians, and are numbered among the company's most valued employees."22

A 1924 fire razed the Windsor shop at 126 Ouellette Ave but the decision was made to rebuild on the same site. The radio and phonograph market, however, soon captured the larger share of the 1930s trade. By 1945 the Grinnell piano had ceased to be made in Windsor, although the Detroit plant operated until 1961. Grinnell used the stencil names Holly, Clayton, Leonard, and Playtona in southwestern Ontario for several years. It also distributed a line of Uxbridge reed organs, c. 1910. (At the time of writing, my son Caleb was restoring one of these eleven-stop organs. Both the Grinnell and Uxbridge names are stencilled on the stop board.)

HADDON HALL – a name used by *MASON & RISCH*.

HAINES BROS. – originally an American piano manufactured by Winter & Company, New York (1898). Made in Canada by Foster-Armstrong, Berlin (Kitchener), Ontario, 1906–24. The line was taken over in late 1924 by *SHERLOCK-MANNING* which continued production until about 1945.

HALLETT & DAVIS – A Boston piano company, 1843–1957. The finish assembly and distribution of its products in Canada were done by *MASON & RISCH*. The M. & R. name generally appeared on the fallboard along with the name of the import.

HANDEL – a name used by *WILLIS*, c. 1910–15. Series in 1913 numbered from 10,500.

HARDY & SONS – a name used by *LESAGE*. Not an American piano, apparently, but no record of the source of the name could be found.

HARMONIC – a name used by *MASON & RISCH*, 1908–11.

HARRINGTON – a line distributed in Canada by *MASON & RISCH*. Originally a New York company, 1871–1960.

HAYDN PIANO MANUFACTURING COMPANY – Montreal, c. 1898.

HEINTSMAN-DALTON COMPANY – Toronto, c. 1835.

HEINTZMAN & COMPANY (see Chapter Six)

GERHARD HEINTZMAN (see Chapter Six)

JOSEPH HERALD – Hamilton, Ontario, c. 1877. Apparently the proprietor of a private workshop, Herald is on file at the Canadian Patent Office for his interesting "Improved Pianoforte" (Patent # 6939, 9 January 1877).

HENRY HERBERT – a piano line named after Henry Herbert Mason, son of Thomas Gabriel Mason, one of three men who established one of Canada's best-known piano companies, *MASON & RISCH*. Durable and of mid-quality, the Henry Herbert line was manufactured in Toronto from 1890 to 1971. (see also *MASON & RISCH*.)

J.W. HERBERT & COMPANY – Montreal, 1835–61. A builder and repairer of pianofortes and organs, Herbert and partner William Dennis imported several instrument lines from Europe and United States to sell side by side with their own. The firm became well known for its active involvement in music publishing during the 1840s.23

H.A. HILLCOAT PIANO COMPANY – Amherst, Nova Scotia. A small piano firm taken over by the newly formed Amherst Pianos Ltd. in 1912. The Hillcoat name was possibly used for several years by the Amherst firm.

HENRY & FRANZ HOERR – Toronto, c. 1891–95.

HOLLY – see Ginnell.

HOMER – a name used by *MASON & RISCH*, 1901–19. The line was apparently revived and the name used again briefly about 1968.

THOMAS D. HOOD – Montreal, c. 1852–77. A former employee at Mead Brothers piano company, Hood took over the firm in 1852. An example of a Hood pianoforte is in the Canadian instrument collection at the Royal Ontario Museum, Toronto. (See also Mead, Mott & Co.)

FREDERICK HUND – Quebec City, 1816. Hund is the earliest known pianoforte maker in Canada. His company became Hund and Seebold until 1824 and later Seebold, Manby & Company up to 1856.

HUND & SEEBOLD – see previous entry.

HENRY G. HUNT – Toronto, c. 1850.

JOSEPH T. HUNT – Saint John, New Brunswick, 1845–55. Manufacturer of square pianofortes.

IMPERIAL PIANO COMPANY – Toronto, 1896–1901. Possibly a subsidiary of Stanley Piano Company. An American firm known as the Imperial Piano Company existed in New York and Chicago from the late 1890s until 1929, but no connection could be established. It is possible that, like most of his contemporaries, Frank Stanley imported and distributed this extra line or acquired the manufacturing rights for Canada.

INTERNATIONAL PIANO COMPANY – Toronto, c. 1928. As with the previous entry, there was an International Piano Company in New York and Chicago at the time, but no connection between these firms has been established. Some sources suggest that Ennis & Company started this firm as a subsidiary c. 1911. Also, records indicate that International bought the assets of Morris and Karn and operated the defunct Listowel, Ontario, factory for about eighteen months between 1926 and 1928. No other information has been located.

JACKSON & COMPANY – Peterborough, Ontario, c. 1889.

JONES & CROSS – Toronto, time unknown, probably prior to 1870.

KARN PIANO COMPANY (see Chapter Six)

THOMAS KATER – Hamilton, Ontario, c. 1875.

C.W. KELLY & SON, J.W. KELLY, KELMONROS – These three names are listed as Canadian manufacturers in the eighth edition of the *Pierce Piano Atlas*; however, research findings indicate C.W. Kelly to have been a retailer only in Guelph. Billed as "one of the largest musical emporiums in Ontario," Kelly's store was a high-volume sales outlet for *BELL* pianos and organs, c. 1890–1910.24 J.W. Kelly Piano Co. Ltd. likewise was not a manufacturer, but a large instrument dealer located at 632 Seymour St Vancouver, during the early 1940s. Kelmonros may have been a briefly used stencil name.

KENNAY & SCRIBNER – Saint John, New Brunswick, c. 1851. The firm seems to have also operated under the name Edmund E. Kennay until 1871. One source lists Kennay & Scribner as a London, England, company that manufactured uprights as early as 1860.

KILGOUR PIANO COMPANY – Hamilton, Ontario, 1888–89. Located at 23 Aurora St. A J.& R. Kilgour pump-organ is in the musical instrument collection at the Huron County Museum, Goderich, Ontario.

KNOTT & SONS – Hamilton, Ontario, c. 1855–1914. A pre-Confederation reporter flattered the Knott company with this 1858 story: "We were so delighted at the excellence of the pianofortes we found there, that we cannot refrain from letting the citizens know our thoughts on the occasion. Mr. Knott – a practical mechanic – was just finishing a cottage piano to be sent to the Provincial Exhibition in Toronto. The very shape of a cottage is something strange in this country, where the less elegant and more cumbersome square is the prevalent form. The Canadian woods have been found admirably adapted for the making of the instrument. From the pine soundingboard to the black walnut case, all the wood Mr. Knott uses is of Canadian growth, and it really gives us confidence in the vastness of our resources when we find this to be possible."[25] The Knott company remained a small, yet quality workshop until the Great War broke out in 1914.

KRANICH & BACH – an old New York company (1864–1981). *MASON & RISCH* had the Canadian rights to their pianos, doing final assembly and distributing the line until about 1925.

KREISLER – a name used by *MASON & RISCH*.

KRYDNER – a name used by *R.S. WILLIAMS*.

LABELLE & CRAIG – Montreal, c. 1854–56. (See also Craig Piano Company.)

LACKNER – a name used by *BELL*.

LAFFARGUE PIANO COMPANY – a New York firm (known as Laffargue-Oktavek at one time). Its name brand was imported by C.W. Lindsay & Company and underwent final cabinet assembly in Montreal. It was distributed throughout Quebec during the early 1900s. The stencil name of "Laverne" may also have been distributed under the Laffargue banner.

J. DONAT LANGELIER – Montreal, 1915–1965. While applying its name to a number of pianos, this firm was not a manufacturer. It distributed L.E.N. Pratte, Strathmore, Sherington, Mansford, and LeClarion pianos.

LANSDOWNE PIANO COMPANY – Toronto, 1886–90. This was a short-lived company but one with a fascinating pedigree. The firm was a collaborative effort between Gerhard Heintzman and Samuel and Albert Nordheimer. The Nordheimer brothers, Samuel and Abraham (Albert's father) had operated a music and instrument business since the early 1840s although they did not produce their own pianos until nearly fifty years later. Gerhard Heintzman, on the other hand, had more demand for his instruments (1877–1885) than he could handle. So the two companies formed the Lansdowne Piano Company, hired a group of Toronto-area tradesmen, and virtually "cleaned up" in the Ontario market-place for five years. Probable associate partners in the venture included Tom Mason and Vincent Risch (later Mason & Risch) and possibly Octavius Newcombe, although these three were already producing pianos of their own at the time. When Heintzman left Lansdowne in 1890 he took most of the key staff with him, establishing the Gerhard Heintzman Piano Company. He used the

Lansdowne name until about 1908. The Nordheimers, bitter at the split, built their own factory and began turning out an excellent line of their own. (see also GERHARD HEINTZMAN, NORDHEIMER, MASON & RISCH, NEWCOMBE)[26]

LARONDA, LARONDE – according to some authorities these two names were manufactured and distributed by WILLIS. But according to Matt Willis (late of the Willis Piano Company) in a 1989 interview, these names were never included in Willis' line of instruments.

LAURILLIARD – Saint John, New Brunswick, c. 1850.

LAVERNE – originally a New York piano, distributed in Canada by C.W. Lindsay, Montreal, c. 1900. (See also Laffargue.)

LAWRENCE PIANO COMPANY – Ottawa, c. 1895.

LAYTON BROS. – Montreal, period unknown.

LEACH – location and period unknown.

LEADER PIANOS – Toronto, 1919–22.

LECLARION – a name used by Langelier.

LEEMING – see Gourlay, Winter & Leeming.

LEGARE (ROYAL KING) – possibly a name used by Langelier.

LEONARD – see Grinnell.

LESAGE PIANOS LTD. (see Chapter Six)

LESAGE & PICHÉ – see LESAGE.

H.A. LEVERMAN & COMPANY – see Williams & Leverman Piano Forte Manufactory.

LEWIS PIANOS – Vancouver (1044 Granville St), c. 1940. May possibly have been a distributor only.

C.W. LINDSAY & COMPANY – Montreal, 1877– c. 1950. A large Montreal piano dealer, Lindsay acquired the Quebec distribution rights for HEINTZMAN (1883), NORDHEIMER (1897), Martin-Orme (1909), and Foisy (1914) among others. Instruments bearing the Lindsay name were manufactured by LESAGE and Craig, c. 1903–42.

THE LISZT – a name used by Stanley, c. 1908. (See also Stanley Piano Company.)

Figure 111. Ad from the British Columbia and Yukon Directory, 1940, p. 2145.

LODGE PIANOS – Edmonton, period unknown. While some sources list Lodge as a distinct company, it seems more probable that the firm was just a western distributor.

LONDON & STERLING – a name used by Archambault.

LONSDALE PIANO COMPANY – Toronto, c. 1915–22.

McCARTHY & DAVIS – Saint John, New Brunswick, c. 1883.

McMILLAN & COMPANY – Kingston, Ontario, c. 1905. Not to be confused with the McMullan company (also Kingston), this was a distinctly separate firm. Serial #1801 used about 1905.

R. McMULLAN & COMPANY – Kingston, Ontario, c. 1897. McMullan is credited with an 1897 patent for a unique piano-tuning pin. The screw pin was conical in shape and designed to enter the wrest plank from behind, supposedly for the purpose of giving greater stability and permanence to the pin position and therefore also providing greater tuning retention. The McMullen company was eventually taken over by Gourlay, Winter & Leeming, which used its name for several years.

J. MAAS PIANO COMPANY – A lone craftsman, Maas is credited with the first upright pianos to be manufactured in Berlin (Kitchener), Ontario. In 1852, in a large brick building on Foundry St, Maas, a former woodworker, set up shop in a few square feet in a sunny, second storey gable end. It appears that Maas was content filling only local demands for his instruments. The records of the Waterloo Historical Society list three of his early customers as Charles Ahrens, Henry Huber, and Charles Hendry, all from nearby Conestoga.

W.H. MANBY – Montreal, 1857–61. (See also Seebold & Manby; Hund & Seebold.)

MANSFORD – a name used by Langelier.

MARSHALL & WENDELL – see Berlin Piano & Organ Company.

MARTIN-ORME PIANO COMPANY – Scottish immigrant James Lawrence Orme founded a music company in Ottawa in 1861 that was to continue close to 120 years. Known originally as J.L. Orme & Sons, the firm had branch stores in Brockville and Kingston, Ontario. As a publishing house, it promoted Canadian composers, including the works of Orme's son George. About 1902 a former *HEINTZMAN* craftsman, Owain Martin, entered partnership with the Ormes and together they started their own piano manufactory, which operated until 1924. But from that year onward, Orme pianos were made by the *LESAGE* plant in Montreal. Four generations of Ormes had maintained this truly family firm from 1861 to 1979.[27]

Serial numbers 1902–24

1902 – 1,000	1904 – 2,700	1906 – 3,000
1908 – 3,900	1910 – 4,500	1915 – 6,700
1917 – 7,700	1919 – 8,400	1921 – 9,000
1922 – 9,300	1923 – 9,600	1924 – 10,000

MASON & RISCH (see Chapter Six)

MEAD, MOTT & COMPANY – Montreal, c. 1827–53. The firm also appears to have been located for a time in Toronto and may have had as many as seven name changes over the years. (Helmut Kallmann's notes in the *Encyclopedia of Music in Canada*, p. 611, provide some fine background.)[28]

MEHLIN & SON – a New York piano assembled in Toronto and sold by Mason & Risch, c. 1905. The fallboard decal read "Mehlin & Sons, New York-Toronto."

MENDELSSOHN PIANO COMPANY – Founded in 1892 in Toronto by Henry Durke and David M. Best, this firm produced several lines of fine-quality pianos until 1924. The latter partner formed D.M. Best Company (1894), a manufacturer and distributor of piano strings, parts, and accessories, and no doubt the most popular supply house for Canadian piano tuners up to the present. (The current owners operate as D.M. Best, 49-6A The Donway West, Suite 416, Don Mills, Ontario). Durke continued the Mendelssohn operation until its takeover in 1919 by *BELL* of Guelph. Bell used the name until c. 1934 when it in turn was bought out by *LESAGE*. Lesage used the Mendelssohn name until 1970.

Serial numbers
1900 – 3,000   1905 – 5,000   1910 – 7,300
1915 – 9,000   1920 – 25,000   1924 – 28,000

OSWALD MICHAUD – a partner with Eculide and Jérémie David, Montreal, c. 1922–3, Michaud was indeed a talented Canadian instrument craftsman. An electric piano known as the "Sonobel" was patented by Michaud in 1937. In an article from *Petit Journal* (Montreal), 20 May 1951, the inventor described it as being able to give "a whole new colour to the sound texture – powerful bass notes, and crystal clear high notes – and is suitable for the whole range of piano literature, early, classical or modern." Michaud was also the regular piano tuner for the Montreal studios of the CBC until the late 1950s.[29] (See also Sonobel.)

HENRY F. MILLER – Boston piano assembled and sold in Toronto by Mason & Risch, c. 1905. The fallboard decal read "Henry F. Miller, Boston-Toronto."

FRANCIS MILLIGAN – Quebec City, c. 1844–64. A brother (or son), George, was also involved in the business.

THE MINUET – a model name (not stencilled on the instrument) used by *LESAGE*, c. 1978–86.

MINX – a 36"-high, 85-note piano originally manufactured in England. *SHERLOCK-MANNING* acquired the Canadian rights to this instrument in 1937 and made over 1,000 that year. With an underslung action, its compactness made it extremely popular for apartment dwellers. Unfortunately, about two years into production, Canada's dry winter climate exposed the fact that these little pianos would not stay in tune. Sherlock-Manning ordered a massive recall approaching 80 per-cent of the total production run. The line was a financial disaster for the already troubled company.[30]

GEORGE & WILLIAM MOIR – Halifax, c. 1852.

MORRIS PIANO COMPANY (see Chapter Six)

MOZART PIANO COMPANY – Toronto, c. 1912–20. Taken over by National Piano Company about 1918.

MOZART SYMPHONY – a name used by *NEWCOMBE*.

MULHOLLAND-NEWCOMBE – a shortlived partnership between well known Toronto piano maker Octavius Newcombe and a Mr Mulholland, c. July 1912.

WILLIAM MUTH – Montreal, 1876. From a patent drawing filed on 28 June 1876, it appears this was a distinct company. Muth's "Tone Diminishing Pedal" was a "first" for Canadian square pianos of the period. No record of the demise of the company could be found.

NATIONAL PIANO COMPANY – Toronto, c. 1915–29. It absorbed the Mozart Piano Company about 1918.

Figure 112. "Muth's Tone Diminishing Pedal" (Patent #6315), filed by William Muth, Montreal, 17 July 1876.

NEWCOMBE PIANO COMPANY (see Chapter Six)

NEW KAUFFMAN – a name used by Uxbridge Piano Company.

NITSCHKE PIANO COMPANY – Started in London, Ontario, in 1869, this small firm is typical of scores of short-lived piano businesses that catered to local markets. John Nitschke's company appears to have done reasonably well in London and Middlesex County for a few years and by 1872 he had built what was known as the "Nitschke Block" on the northeast corner of Dundas and Wellington streets. This included a dozen or so stores, his residence, and a factory behind it all. Employing about ten men and making square pianos only, Nitschke served the immediate and local consumer. An ad in the 1877 London city directory argued that "import duty, freight and profits charged by piano traders and their agents might be saved to the buyer by purchasing a Nitschke Piano." John Nitschke died in 1884, the property was sold, and the business ended.[31]

NORDHEIMER PIANO COMPANY (see Chapter Six)

O'NEILL BROS. – Toronto, c. 1844.

ONTARIO PIANO COMPANY – Toronto, c. 1928.

J.L. ORME & SONS – see Martin-Orme.

OSHAWA ORGAN & MELODEON COMPANY – Oshawa, Ontario, 1871. Located in the "Sons of Temperance" Hall, Simcoe St, Oshawa, until June 1873.[32] (See *DOMINION ORGAN & PIANO CO.*, and Darley & Robinson.)

OSHAWA PIANO & CABINET COMPANY – Oshawa, period unknown. Likely before 1870.

R.S. OWEN & SON – Quebec City, c. 1840.

PALACE GRAND – a name used by Uxbridge Piano Company.

PALMER PIANO COMPANY – Uxbridge, Ontario, 1907–09. A "flash in the pan" company, started by several former Uxbridge Piano Company employees. An Uxbridge newspaper article of 12 September 1907 indicates that the town issued a debenture in the amount of $25,000 to help set up the factory close to a Grand Trunk Railway siding. Hopes of employing up to 100 men had been entertained. Fourteen months later things looked quite dismal and the Mendelssohn Piano Company (Toronto) made overtures with regard to renting the factory and buying the stock. By March 1909 Palmer was history.[33]

PEPIN & SONS – Edmonton, period unknown.

PERCIVAL PIANO COMPANY – Ottawa, c. 1918.

J.M. PFEIFFER – Quebec City, c. 1849.

Figure 113. The Palmer Piano Company building, Uxbridge, Ontario. The premises were later occupied by the Gold Medal Furniture Company.

H. & J. PHILIPS – Halifax, c. 1845–59. The Philips brothers had come from Hamburg, Germany, about 1845 and were the first to manufacture a piano in Nova Scotia. Sir John Harvey, the lieutenant-governor of the colony honoured the enterprise by purchasing its first instrument. Taken over by W. Fraser & Sons. (See also Brockley & Co. and Williams & Leverman)[34]

PLAOLA PIANO COMPANY – Oshawa. Manufactured player pianos only. Possibly a subsidiary of *R.S. WILLIAMS* c. 1910.

PLAYTONA – see Grinnell.

POITRAS BROS. – Quebec City, period unknown.

L.E.N. PRATTE – see next entry.

THE PRATTE PIANO COMPANY – Montreal, c. 1875–1926. Louis-Étienne-Napoléon Pratte opened a small music store in Montreal about 1875. His brother, Antonio, who spent seven years apprenticing with *DOMINION ORGAN AND PIANO COMPANY* in Bowmanville, Ontario, joined him in 1889 and the pair soon produced their first upright piano. As an inventor (and patent owner) of several imaginative damper and sounding-board designs, Antonio was quite active in securing newly developed American and European patent rights, incorporating them into the line that became known as the L.E.N. Pratte piano. An ad from *L'Art Musical* of 1896, as reproduced in *Encyclopedia of Music In Canada*, describes the L.E.N. Pratte instrument as possessing "artistic qualities not found in US or European pianos. [Our] system guarantees in addition to the rarest musical qualities, maximum solidity and durability in extreme climates." The Pratte company turned out its first grand in 1912. By 1926, however, business was bad. The company merged with J. Donat Langelier in that year.[35]

PRELUDE – a model name (not stencilled on the instrument) used by *LESAGE* c. 1978–86.

PRESTON – a stencil-name piano distributed in Canada by *MASON & RISCH* in 1912. Originally a New York piano made by Kohler & Campbell.

PRINCE PIANO COMPANY – Toronto, c. 1885–1914. The company may also have been known as Prince and Dodds, and Walls, Prince and Wilks.

PRINCESS – a name used by both *R.S. WILLIAMS* and *MORRIS PIANO COMPANY*, although no connection between the two has been established.

PRINCESS ROYAL – a name used by Amherst, c. 1910.

QUIDOZ PIANO LTÉE – A Quebec piano company established at Ste Thérèse-de-Blainville in 1897 and originally known as *Sénécal et Quidoz*. The principals were Joseph Sénécal and Georges Quidoz. The former had learned the piano trade as a technician at Thomas F.G. Foisy's (Canadian Piano Company) during the early 1890s and later with Lesage & Piché. By the late 1920s, the Quidoz firm was offering nine different models including a grand and a player piano. The name Gerhard was used from 1955–57. The company survived, though modestly, until 1966.[36]

RAINER & COMPANY – Whitby, Ontario, 1866, then possibly moved to Guelph, c. 1872. Used Dominion as a brand name.

RAPPE, WEBER & CO. – Kingston, Ontario, c. 1868–69. (See also *WEBER/WORMWITH*.)

REED BROS. – Toronto, period unknown. One source lists their retail outlet as 257 King St.

ISAAC REINHARDT – Montreal, c. 1846.

J. REYNER – Kingston, c. 1870. (See also *WEBER/WORMWITH*.)

REYNOLDS & DUFFETT – Toronto, c. 1849.

ROBINSON & SON PIANOS – Edmonton. Possibly just a western dealer.

J.T. ROWE – Toronto, time unknown.

SAINT-SAENS – a name used by Colonial Piano Company, Ste-Thérèse-de-Blainville, Quebec, c. 1920.

SCHUBERT – a name used by *R.S. WILLIAMS*.

SCHUMANN – originally a name used by *BELL*, but, following its takeover by *LESAGE* in 1934, the latter used the name for a number of years.

SCHUMANN PIANO COMPANY – Toronto, period unknown.

SEEBOLD, MANBY & COMPANY – see Frederick Hund.

SÉNÉCAL ET QUIDOZ – see Quidoz Piano Ltée.

J.W. SHAW & CO. – Montreal, c. 1905. (See also Beethoven.)

SHERLINGTON – a name used by Langelier.

SHERLOCK-MANNING (see Chapter Six)

B. SLADE – Halifax, c. 1832.

SMALL & McARTHUR – see Thomas Boyd.

F.G. SMITH – a New York piano packaged and distributed 1874–78 by *DOMINION ORGAN & PIANO COMPANY*.

W.H. SNYDER – see Berlin Piano & Organ Company.

SOLO PLAYER PIANO COMPANY – Located on the north side of High St in Clinton, Ontario, the firm was incorporated in November of 1913. German craftsman Paul Van Rohl was the principal technical mind in the operation, with Tom "Sliver" McNeil heading up the finishing department and J.W. Moore as head tuner. Financiers H.E. Boyd and Fred Hill were also on the board of directors. The company appears to have failed by about 1915, whereupon "Sliver" McNeil returned to his former job down the street at *W. DOHERTY & CO.* 37

SONATA – a model name (not stencilled on the instrument) used by *LESAGE* c. 1978–86.

SONOBEL – an electric piano developed by Oswald Michaud in 1937. Used in assorted CBC radio productions and in Charlottetown in 1939 at an official reception for King George VI, the invention unfortunately was not commercially successful. Although numerous noted pianists praised the instrument, the Second World War and a shortage of materials prevented further development. 38 (See also Oswald Michaud.)

LEWIS NELSON SOPER – Guelph, Ontario. Although this has not been confirmed, Soper may have been employed by *BELL*. He is listed here as a separate entry because of his outstanding inventiveness. Between 27 March 1900 and 23 March 1909, he was granted at least seven different patents on improved piano actions. His highly detailed drawings and modifications that improved with each successive patent, made him indeed a rare talent and no doubt a prize to whoever employed him. No record of a distinct Soper piano could be found.39

SOVEREIGN – a name used by Palmer Piano Company in 1908.

ROLAND M. SQUIRE – Montreal, c. 1895.

Figure 114. Stanley iron-plate casting. The entire top line of the casting reads "Diploma and Honorable Mention, Chicago 1893." Apart from the hand-painted lines and floral designs, a colourful Stanley company crest was also stencilled onto the plate.

Figure 115. Ornate chromed casting on a Stanley piano (c. 1898).

STANDARD PIANO COMPANY – Toronto, c. 1898.

THE STANLEY PIANO COMPANY OF TORONTO LIMITED – Although not a major Canadian producer nor an adventurous exporter, Frank Stanley took pride in detail. His piano-case construction was meticulous. Even where unobserved, finely painted pin-stripe lines and *art deco* stylings kissed the dark interiors. A rarity in the trade of the time, a personalized chrome kickplate framed the foot-pedal trio on each instrument. Formed in Toronto (or possibly Peterborough) in 1890, the operation remained fairly small, producing only a few hundred pianos each year. An 1893 Chicago Trade Show award was a major coup for the new company, Stanley having it proudly cast into his iron-frame plates. The firm's only known takeover occurred in 1922, when Stanley acquired the assets of the Cecilian Piano Company. Two years later, however, the firm failed. *MASON & RISCH* picked up the stock at auction.

STEINBACH – a name used by *MASON & RISCH*, c. 1904–11.

JOHN STEPHENSON – Montreal, c. 1848.

STERLING – a name used by Canadian Piano Company, later by *MASON & RISCH*, and still later (c. 1935) by *SHERLOCK-MANNING*.

STEVENSON & COMPANY – see *WEBER/WORMWITH*.

STRATHMORE – a name used by Langelier.

SUMNER & BREBNER – Founded in Ingersoll, Ontario, in February 1906, the Sumner & Brebner Piano Company was a late starter in an industry on the decline. Brothers Ernest and Sidney Sumner and James Brebner (and possibly Hubert Brebner) had been employed at *EVANS BROS. PIANO COMPANY*. Ernest Sumner, who had been an actions regulator with the Evans firm, appears to have been the "brains" of the business and organized the company in a small, yellow-brick factory at the corner of Hall and Kings streets in Ingersoll.[40] A year after production began, a local paper noted that the Sumners were "expert workmen of extensive experience and they produce a very fine class of instrument which sells readily on its merits." Although a player piano was also included in its line about 1910, the company's accomplishments apparently did not allow it to succeed much past 1915.[41] (See also *EVANS BROTHERS*.)

Serial numbers include

1906 – 500	1907 – 750	1908-800
1909 – 1,000	1910 – 2,000	1911 – 2,600
1912 – 2,900	1913 – 3,100	

C.L. THOMAS ORGAN & PIANO COMPANY – Charles Lewis Thomas was born in Thornbury, Gloucestershire, England, on 4 May 1828. The eldest of thirteen children, he arrived in Canada with his father, John Morgan Thomas, in 1832. Educated in Toronto and encouraged by his instrument-making father to enter the trade, Thomas set up his own organ and piano business in Hamilton in 1855, just a few months after his marriage. About 1886 a Hamilton publication referred to a Thomas instrument as "a piano not merely of fine glossy exterior or made for cheap use, but an instrument in which the purchaser might invest and feel satisfied that, with fair treatment, it would last a family for a lifetime, and always be prized as a valuable possession."[42] At age sixty-two, however, C.L. Thomas was stricken with a disease that claimed his life a year later on 4 October 1891. He had been an extremely active municipal politician and respected businessman, and the whole of Hamilton mourned his death. The business is believed to have ceased in 1892.[43]

THOMAS ORGAN & PIANO COMPANY – John Morgan Thomas, an Irish immigrant to Canada, began making small melodeons in Montreal in 1832. On his move to Toronto in 1839, he entered into a partnership with Alexander Smith, the pair having acquired an important patent for a metallic piano frame and pin-block assembly. The new invention claimed to eliminate the case strain which, resulting from the Canadian climate, had previously necessitated constant retuning.

One of Thomas' five sons, Edward G. Thomas, had been actively involved in his father's music business but decided to strike out on his own in the mid-1870s. A move to Woodstock in 1875 put three organ companies in the small Oxford County community – the others being New Dominion Organ Factory and Miller & Karn.

The following year, one of Edward Thomas' reed organs won a bronze medal and commisioner's diploma at a large trade show at the Centennial Exhibition in Philadelphia. Many international buyers had been present and had noted the fine quality of the Thomas product. With this success, the Thomas Organ Company continued to grow steadily. By 1885 a large new brick factory was constructed at the junction of the Grand Trunk and Canadian Pacific Railway lines and pianos were introduced to the Thomas roster.

On the death of Ed Thomas in 1891, James Dunlop and J.G. Short acquired controlling interest, with Dunlop eventually gaining sole control by 1895. At that time the name Thomas Organ & Piano Company was officially coined. With Dunlop at the helm (and later his sons John and William), a successful export market was developed. A report from the 1 July 1901 issue of the *Woodstock Sentinel-Review* stated, "The goods now have a worldwide reputation. Their quality is a *sine qua non* for perfection, and it can safely be said that no single firm has done more to foster a taste for high class instruments and to supply this demand than the Thomas Company. The Thomas

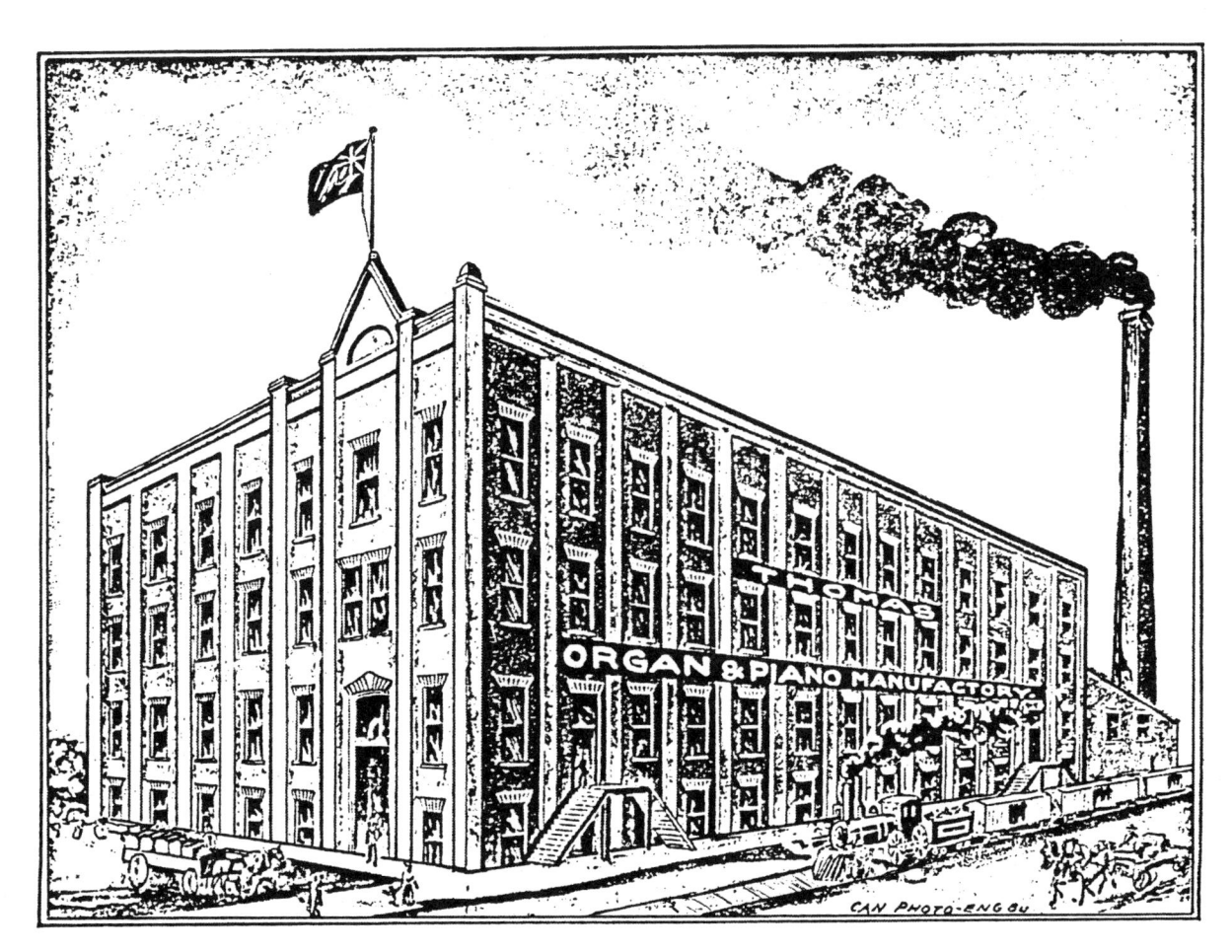

Figure 116. The Thomas Organ & Piano Company, Woodstock, c. 1897.

employees are a well paid and devoted band of workmen. The good fellowship among them has for years been very noticeable."

With approximately 90 employees at the turn of the century, 150 reed organs, 1,000 piano stools, and several dozen pianos a month were produced. And while no record of exact piano production has survived, it appears that when war broke out in 1914 materials and demand for the Thomas product were greatly diminished. A drift to bedroom-furniture production kept the business afloat for another decade or so, but the company finally closed during the 1930s.[44]

The Thomas name has meant much to the Canadian piano and organ industry. Edward's four brothers were similarly involved in the trade. Charles L. Thomas founded the Western Pianoforte Manufactory of Canada in Hamilton. John L. Thomas was in the employ of *BELL PIANO AND ORGAN CO.* until the 1920s. Thomas L. Thomas worked for *R.S. WILLIAMS* in both Toronto and Oshawa. And Frank J. Thomas was a private piano builder.

WILLIAM TOWNSEND – Hamilton, Ontario (or possibly Toronto), c. 1848. Young Richard Williams (later founder of *R.S. WILLIAMS PIANO CO.*) worked as an apprentice in this small melodeon shop.

UXBRIDGE PIANO COMPANY – Uxbridge, Ontario, a small community northeast of Toronto, has never been bashful about its artistic residents. L.M. Montgomery lived here from 1911 to 1926. Artist David Milne called Uxbridge home during the 1940s. And the community was long the home of pianist Glenn Gould's parents and grandparents.

Back in 1873, a desire for "the finer things in a cultured society" led a group of twenty-one Uxbridge businessmen to from a joint-stock company known as the Uxbridge Cabinet Organ Co. Under the direction of John McGuire, the small firm flourished. By 1878 twenty-five men were turning out as many a thirty organs a month. The following year a piano department was added and in February 1884 a record order for 100 instruments made the whole town feel good. Business was still flying high a decade or so later when an apparent lull in sales sent the company into a tail-spin. Liquidation took place on 11 April 1895. By the early years of the new century, however, new life had been breathed into the old business and the Uxbridge Piano & Organ Co. was off and running again, with fifteen of its

Figure 117. Uxbridge Cabinet Organ Co., Uxbridge, Ontario, c. 1902. This frame building was destroyed by fire in 1907. Afterwards, a new brick structure was constructed on the site.

models being presented at the Toronto Exhibition in August 1906. Still, the decision had been made to restrict the labour force to just fifteen employees.

Despite reorganization of its marketing and sales strategies, and an extraordinarily successful selling effort in 1907 by its travelling salesman, Hillary McGuire, the company began to fall apart. By mid-1914 the Uxbridge Piano & Organ Company was no more.[45]

VERSAILLES – a model name (though not stencilled on the instrument) used by *LESAGE* c. 1978–86. Two styles, the Queen Anne and the French Provincial, were offered.

WADSWORTH – a name piano distributed in Canada by *MASON & RISCH*, c. 1914-16.

WAGNER, ZEIDLER & CO. – Toronto, c. 1889. Manufactured actions for square pianos but possibly made a limited number of their own instruments.

WALLS, PRINCE & WILKS – Toronto, c. 1885-90. Serial #1381 about 1888.

S.R. WARREN – Samuel Warren was a native of Rhode Island who settled in Montreal about 1836. A noted organ builder throughout Quebec and Ontario for many years, he apparently manufactured a few pianofortes about 1845. About 1896, several years after the firm had come into the hands of his son, Samuel Prowse Warren, it was sold to *D.W. KARN & COMPANY*, Woodstock, Ontario. The name Karn-Warren appeared on some instruments until around 1911, when Frank, Charles, and Mansfield Warren (grandsons of old Samuel R. Warren) started the Warren Church Organ Company.[46] (See also *D.W. KARN & COMPANY*.)

WEBER PIANO COMPANY (& WORMWITH) (see Chapter Six)

WERLICH BROS. – An adventurous young man who possessed neither horse nor the price of a train ticket, set out on foot from Preston, Ontario, on a hot July morning in 1901. His destination was Buffalo, New York, some ninety miles from his hometown. Several weeks later, travel-worn, John Werlich secured his heart's desire – employment at a famous piano-manufacturing company.

Werlich had a headful of ideas and a love of music, and also had acquired a measure of skill as a cabinet maker in Preston. Within a few short years, he was made superintendent at the Chase and Baker Piano Company, and he telegraphed his family in Preston with the news. A few weeks later his brother William and friends Louis Gillow and Fred Eitel arrived in Buffalo and were happy to accept employment at Chase and Baker. But the memories and lure of their hometown soon rushed in on these young men, and by 1908 they had all returned to Preston – heads swimming with grand ideas of starting their own business.

While at the Chase and Baker operation, Werlich *et al* had worked on a relatively new invention – the piano player. And between them, several design modifications and new ideas had surfaced, sufficient to fuel their hopes of starting a piano-player industry in Ontario.

Obtaining the old Crown Furniture factory in Preston, the four men began a manufacturing operation based solely on the production of piano players. Soon, however, their plant location was considered less than favourable. The piano-player components demanded the use of small leather bellows and valves. Their low-lying factory was just too humid. The leather mechanisms worked well on the assembly line, but, once shipped to retail outlets or customers' homes, the subsequent dryness caused shrinkage. The instrument moaned, groaned, squeaked, and sucked. The reputation of the Prestion piano player plummeted.[47]

Several moves to more suitable quarters were tried. Twice fire reduced the company to "square one." And by 1912 or so, the advent of the instrument that was both a piano and capable of doing the work of the piano player had reduced the Werlich product to redundancy.

By 1916 John and William Werlich, as principal owners, had determined that the musical-instrument business was either too competitive or simply not their forte. A line of wooden toboggans, skis, sleds, and wagons was begun. With tricycles and bicycles added later, the firm – then known as Canadian Wagon & Novelty Company – survived until 1968.

A sad footnote, however, accompanies the story of the Werlich piano players. About 1950 Reginald Werlich, a son of the late John, obtained two of the only known surviving piano players that had been produced in his father's factory. Storing these in a vacant wing of his own manufacturing complex, he hoped some day to restore the contraptions. How sad he must have been when several years later he discovered that workmen had chopped them up and fed them to the factory boiler furnace.

WESTERN PIANO MANUFACTORY OF CANADA – a company established in Hamilton by Charles L. Thomas, c. 1856. (See also *D.W. KARN & CO.* and C.L. Thomas Organ & Piano Co.)

WHALEY-ROYCE PIANO COMPANY – This Toronto company, later noted more as a dealer in band instruments and sheet music, manufactured its own pianos briefly about 1905. Its ads boasted a seven-year guarantee and a piano that was "unexcelled in tone, faultless in mechanical construction, original and elegant in design." A showroom was located at 158 Yonge St.[48]

R.S. WILLIAMS & COMPANY (see Chapter Six)

WILLIAMS & LEVERMAN – A dimly lit, clapboard building on Upper Water St, Halifax, was the birthplace of this company in 1859. Manufacturing a few melodeons and square pianos, William Williams and Henry A. Leverman quickly gained both the ears and the money of city music lovers. Leverman had learned the trade as early as 1846 with Nova Scotia's first pianoforte makers, H. & J. Philips.

By 1871 a move to larger quarters at 11–15 Carleton Street was dictated since this young Halifax company had expanded to more than twenty workmen. Making cottage (upright) pianos by this time, Williams and Leverman found the raw materials of Nova Scotia ideally suited to their needs. As *Halifax and Its Business* stated in 1876, "In the essential qualities of resonant and liquid tones, together with strength and durability, and beauty of finish, the Pianos of this firm will not suffer by comparison with any imported instru-

Figure 118. Wiiliams & Leverman piano forte factory, Halifax, c. 1876.

ment. The principal portions of the wood work are of native woods, which are superior for the purpose and better adapted to this climate than foreign woods." [49]

Williams & Leverman, despite their natural advantages and talents, do not appear to have survived beyond 1890. H.A. Leverman & Co. may have been the successor to this firm c. 1890–97.

WILLIS & BAKER – London, Ontario, 1868–80. Although primarily a manufacturer of reed organs and melodeons, Horace A. Willis and John H. Baker employed workmen who produced several large pipe-organs. The firm, located at 237–239 King St, also made and sold its own square pianos.[50]

WILLIS & COMPANY (see Chapter Six)

H.C. WILSON – a name used by *WEBER/WORMWITH* as early as 1901 and up to 1928.

WINNIPEG PIANO COMPANY – Winnipeg, Manitoba, period unknown.

WINTER – see Gourlay, Winter & Leeming.

WORMWITH – see *WEBER PIANO COMPANY*.

WRIGHT PIANO COMPANY LTD. – A retail business that started selling boots and shoes in Strathroy, Ontario, in 1865, and evolved into a piano manufactory by 1908. James Wright, founder, passed on his love of music and the piano to his five sons, all of whom were at one time involved in the business. Although piano construction ended in April 1920 – by which time total production of the high-quality Wright piano had reached more than 4,000 units – the name Wright Piano Company survived until the early 1930s. An orchestra, made up of four Wright brothers and two other musicians, gained wide acclaim in southwestern Ontario during that decade.[51]

Figure 119. Wright Piano Company orchestra, c. 1932. Left to right: Bert Thomas, Donald Wright, William Wright, H. Wilkinson, Ernest Wright, Clark Wright.

CHAPTER EIGHT

How Old Is My Piano?

Please consider the following facts:

~ Tens of millions of pianos have been manufactured world-wide during the past 200 years.

~ Global production for one year alone (1911) was estimated at 650,000 units.

~ Worldwide production has not fallen off in more recent years. According to a 1970 United Nations survey piano production for that year was 756,000 instruments, with Japan being the largest producer.

~ In the United States alone, more than 5,000 individual brand-name pianos have been marketed since 1880.

~ Canadian piano production indicates that close to 240 different company brand- and stencil-name pianos have been made since 1816.

~ One company, Bell Piano and Organ Co., Guelph, claimed to have manufactured 170,000 instruments by 1928.

~Many pianos have been refinished, thereby removing original fallboard decals, stencils, and identification.

~ With only a few exceptions, the piano manufacturers of Canada were not compelled to hire record keepers or statisticians. Most company documentation vanished as easily as the sawdust that was swept from their factory floors.

Because of all of this, determining the age of a Canadian piano can be a very formidable task if one tries to locate identifying marks, company records, or product serial numbers. Fires, floods, disasters of other kinds, the "paper drives" of the Second World War, and the fact that most industry people have been businessmen rather than historians has led to a lamentable lack of documentation on Canadian pianos.

There are literally thousands of letters of request on file at libraries and historical societies across the country seeking information relative to certain piano manufacturers. The local history expert at the Woodstock (Ontario) public library notes that they have "more requests for information about the Karn and Thomas piano factories [Woodstock companies] than anything else."

Although suppliers of piano components and tools, such as the D.M. Best Co. or Otto Higel Co. (both of Toronto) did periodically publish limited piano serial numbers to assist tuners and technicians, a comprehensive listing of Canadian piano numbers has never been made.

In California, however, a man who has earned the name "Mr. Piano" provides a publication that may help those with serious inquiries.

Bob Pierce started what was to be a lifelong career in the piano business in 1927 at the age of fourteen. While he was working as an office boy for the then largest music retailer in the world, Jenkins Music Co., Kansas City, Missouri, Bob's fascination with the piano and with collecting historical facts and figures was soon manifest. Twenty years later, Pierce obtained copyright ownership of the authoritative collection of American piano serial numbers that had been catalogued by N.E. Michel. The resulting 1947 publication was the first edition of the now famous *Pierce Piano Atlas*.[1]

Having made many round-the-world trips and regularly corresponding with several thousand people in the piano and organ industry, Pierce has produced a publication that is indeed authoritative and comprehensive. Of the 11,600 brand names and companies listed in the 1982 (eighth) edition, 157 are Canadian. Serial numbers are available for twenty-two of these.

Bell	Karn	Sherlock-Manning
Columbia	Lesage	Steinbach & Dreher
Doherty	Lindsay	Stevenson
Gerhard Heintzman		Mason & Risch
Sumner & Brebner		
Gourlay, Winter & Leeming		Newcombe Weber
Nordheimer	Williams	
Heintzman	J.L. Orme	Willis
Henry Herbert	Prince	

In this book, known serial numbers that have come from authentic firsthand Canadian records are listed with each manufacturer. The piano serial numbers appearing with some

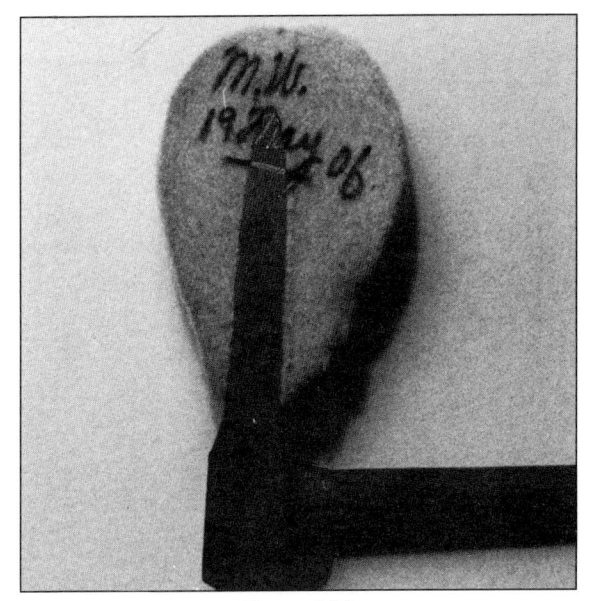

Figure 120.

Figure 121.

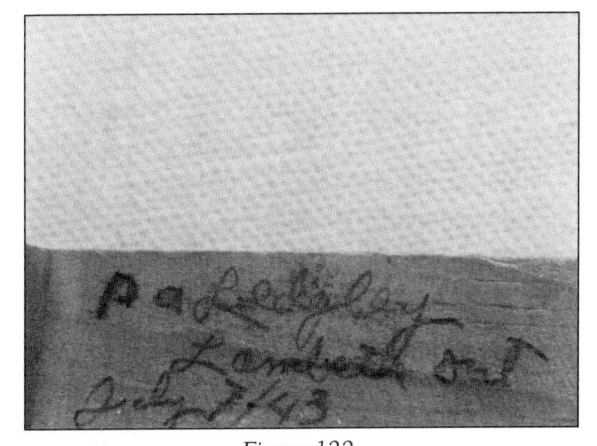

Figure 122.

Canadian pianos will help approximate the year of manufacture. However, since these numbers have been gathered from many different sources – public libraries, archives, private individuals, and piano tradesmen – no doubt discrepancies abound. Still if you know the serial number of your piano (usually stamped on the sounding board or engraved on the iron-frame plate), it is generally possible by using the Pierce Atlas or this publication to isolate the year in which the instrument was manufactured back to 1900. For nineteenth century pieces back to 1880, the date of production can usually be narrowed down to within two or three years.

The Pierce Atlas numbers have not been noted here as they are within the copyright that covers that publication. While wishing me well on my project, Bob Pierce reluctantly would not allow the verbatim reproduction of his collected Canadian numbers, stating that "these facts are my only stock in trade." His point is well taken.[2]

The *Pierce Piano Atlas* is a great reference work for any serious keyboard musician, tuner, dealer, or antique buff. The ninth edition is scheduled for publication this year. (See also the headings in Chapter Seven for "Classic" and "Craig Piano Company" for additional points concerning why consecutive serial numbering cannot always be viewed as a reliable guide for accurate dating or production quantities.)

Otherwise, your local piano tuner is no doubt your best guide. The D.M. Best Piano Atlas (first published in Toronto in 1894 – available only to piano tuners and technicians – may provide the most reliable Canadian serial-number identifications. For the modest cost of a tuning, one of these qualified professionals will no doubt be able to peg your piano to within a few months of its actual construction date.

Efforts to identify a piano by means of case or cabinet design may allow generalized period dating but cannot be considered a guide to isolating specific production years. Piano companies were furniture makers; entire departments were devoted to the manufacture of keybed and bench legs only. Louis XIV, colonial, Queen Ann, French Provincial, art nouveau styles, or what have you, graced all manner of pianos from almost all companies. The wide music desk (the board against which your music rests) was often the scene of artful Roman scrolls, medieval roses or fluting, Chippendale honeysuckles, wreaths, festoons, or rococo border designs. And with most firms manufacturing at least three or four models, these "trim" items varied according to consumer tastes and the whims of cabinet designers. Certain leg styles, for instance, might appear for three of four years, vanish for the next two decades, and then appear again. Consequently, a certain piano cabinet style tells us nothing about the instrument's specific age.

Just as most new car owners today try to follow professional suggestions regarding service, most new piano owners in the past appreciated the suggestions of dealers concerning regular tuning and inspection programs. And since the tradition of leaving personal marks or initials developed very early in the piano industry, often it is possible to come close to the year of manufacture by examining these "hidden" marks that are no doubt inscribed somewhere on your piano. (See Figures 120, 121, and 122.) Some of these marks will be within your ability to search for and observe. Others may not be visible except to the trained eyes and hands of a skilled piano tuner.

The following chapter includes useful suggestions offered by professional tuners and piano technicians that may further shed light on the probable manufacturer, age, and worth of your old piano. ♪

CHAPTER NINE

Buyer's Guide

After a house and a car, a piano is perhaps the most expensive purchase for an average family. With a new Japanese, Korean, or American piano ranging anywhere from $5,000 to $25,000, many households have opted to buy a used instrument. And considering that as many as a million pianos have been made in Canada in just the past 130 years, many consumers try to find "a good old used upright."

Easier said than done!

As recently as 1982, it was estimated that 40,000 old pianos were discarded annually in the United States alone.[1] While that figure initially seems shockingly high, consider the millions of Model T's and other vintage automobiles that have gone the way of the demolition derby and the scrap-yard. Further, just because an instrument is old does not mean that it is inherently better than a new one.

According to Carl Schmeckel's *The Piano Owners Guide – How to Buy and Care for a Piano*, "at least 80 percent of old, neglected instruments are unqualified junk. Perhaps 18 percent are worthy of complete reconditioning and restoration. The remaining 2 percent, owing to proper care through the years, are still in good condition." So what do you think are your chances of acquiring one from that 2-per-cent group? Or even from the 18-per-cent lot?

With an average of 6,000 parts in most upright pianos, and the reality that – to the uninitiated – these items are as mechanically complicated as a Massey-Ferguson combine, the wisdom in seeking the advice of a qualified piano tuner or technician soon becomes obvious. Most larger centres in Canada will carry *Yellow Pages* listings for piano tuners. One who is associated with the Canadian Association of Piano Tuners, the Piano Tuners Guild of America, or (in Ontario) the Ontario Guild of Piano Technicians should be well qualified and capable of inspecting a used piano prior to purchase.

In the fall of 1989 I conducted a survey of several dozen piano tuners from coast to coast. The following figures emerged from that survey:
– Average fee charged to inspect a used piano for a prospective buyer $ 40.00
– Average fee charged for a piano tuning (repairs and materials extra) $ 62.00

- Complete action overhaul (parts included) $500 – $2,000
- Stripping/refinishing case (average) $1,450
- Average selling price for a Canadian upright (40 years old or more) $1,000

The piano tuners surveyed also made a number of suggestions on what to beware of in a used piano:
- cracked bridges
- rust on strings and tuning pins
- cracked pin block; loose pins
- stains beneath pins (that is, an indi-cation that pin "doping" has been done)
- cracked iron plate or harp
- cracked sounding board if rib separation has occured (but can be acceptable in open areas)
- sounding board loose from cabinet
- felts, and hammers old or moth-eaten
- structural damage to cabinet: broken floor, loose posts, and bracing components, and so on
- in Western Canada: signs of excessive dryness causing unglued frames, cracked and split everywhere
- signs of flood or water damage
- strong musty smell
- anything prior to 1880
- square pianos
- a piano with many missing key tops. Usually an indication that this piano has been neglected for years
- very out of tune piano, action unresponsive, tone dull
- tuning substantially below concert pitch
- evidence that name or serial number has been altered

The following publications have fine information concerning the hunt for a good qualitiy, restorable old piano. They should be available at most larger libraries in Canada.

John Becker, "The Piano in Your Parlour," *Canadian Collector* (May/June 1983), pp. 24 – 26.

Sandra Bernstein, "Piano Lessons," *Ontario Living* (March 1987), pp. 43 – 47.

Evelyn Chau, "There's More to Buying a Piano Than Tickling the Ivories," *Canadian Living* (20 May 1985), p.174.

Susan Gould and Robert Fredricks, *The Offical Price Guide to Music Collectibles*, 1st edition, (House of Collectibles, Inc., Orlando, Florida, 1980), pp. 283 – 89.

Edward J. Julian, "Tips on Buying a Piano," *Canadian Consumer* (February 1980), pp. 14 – 16.

Carl D. Schmeckel, *The Piano Owner's Guide – How to Buy and Care for a Piano* (Charles Scribner's Sons, New York, 1974).

Mary Weins, "Guide to Finding a Vintage Upright," *Canadian Music Magazine* (March/April 1985), pp.20 – 22.

Additionally, some of the publications referred to in the bibliography will serve well in equipping the potential piano buyer with enough knowledge to make an informed decision. Remember! Get the advice of a well-qualified, respected piano tuner or technician before you hand over your cheque. The little extra you pay now will be returned a hundredfold with the enjoyment received from a good old Canadian upright. ♪

CHAPTER TEN

The Organ Makers

There have been many reed and pipe-organ manufacturers in Canada over the years. A most interesting account of this aspect of our past is included in the *Encyclopedia of Music in Canada*, and those desiring further information would be well advised to consult that encyclopedia's bibliography under the headings "Organ Building" (pp.710 – 12) and "Reed Organs" (p. 801).

Reflecting on the demise of the parlour organ in this country, Benjamin Scott observed in 1930 that "one reason for the growing popularity of the piano was that it did not have to be 'pumped', as did the organ. Moreover, as a musical instrument, it was more flexible and adaptable for the expression of the most complex compositions. As the piano became popular, the organ 'went out', largely because there were few organ teachers and musicians were more familiar with the piano, on which they had acquired their skill. After 1910, the piano had practically driven the organ off the market." [1]

As outlined previously, the Canadian piano industry is closely linked to many early organ companies. In many instances the references here are to very small, short-lived companies, (occasionally just individual craftsmen), but they are included for those who may wish to examine further this chapter of Canadian music history. No comprehensive efforts were made to research each company; a few illustrations and photographs are presented at the end of the listing.

The companies are as follows:

Acadia Organ Co., Bridgetown, NS 1878–82
Andrews, C.W. & F.M., Picton, ON 1868
Andrus Brothers Organ Co., London, ON 1847–74
Annapolis Organs, Annapolis, NS 1880
Bagnall & Co., Victoria, BC 1863–85
Daniel Bell Organ Co., Toronto, ON 1881–86
Benson Brothers Co., London, ON 1847
Blatchford Organ Co., Galt, ON 1895
Blythe & Kennedy, Ottawa, ON 1831
Bolton & Baldwin, Winnipeg, MB 1888
Brekels & Matthews, Toronto, ON ?
Abner Brown, Montreal, QC 1848–74
Brunzema Organs, Fergus, ON 1979–
Canada Organ Co., Toronto, ON 1875
Casavant Freres, Montreal, QC 1840–
Richard Coates, Montreal, QC 1848
Coleman & Sons, Toronto, ON ?

Compensating Pipe Organ Co., Toronto, ON 1900–10
Cornwall & Huntingdon, Quebec, City, QC 1889–95
Cowley Church Organ Co., Madoc, ON 1890
Dales & Dalton, Newmarket, ON 1870
R.H. Dalton, Toronto, ON 1869–82
Napoleon Dery, Quebec City, QC 1874
Watson Duchemin, Charlottetown, PI 1850
T. Eaton Co., Toronto – had own name brands from 1904
Ebenezer Organ Co., Clifford, ON 1935
Frazee Organ Comp. NB 1871
Goderich Organ Co., Goderich, ON 1890–1910
Guelph Melodeon Co., Guelph, ON 1869–71
Guelph Organs, Guelph, ON ?
Hager & Voght, Preston, ON 1837 (Hamilton, 1849)
J.C. Hallman Co., Kitchener, ON 1949–76
A.S. Hardy & Co., Guelph, ON 1874
Hay & Co., Woodstock, ON 1876
James Hepburn, Picton, NS 1881
John Jackson Organ Co., Guelph, ON 1872–83
Keates Organ Co., Acton, ON 1945-
F. & R. Kilgour, Hamilton c. 1885
Knoch Organ Co., London, ON 1954–
Limbrecht Organ Co., Preston, ON 1849
Lye Organ Co., Toronto, ON 1873–1934
McLeod, Wood & Co., Guelph, ON 1869–72
R. McLeod & Co., London, ON 1872–75
Malhoit & Co., Simcoe, ON 1875
Charles Mee Organs, Kingston, ON 1870
Miller Organ Co., Woodstock, ON 1867
Minshall Organ Co., London, ON c. 1939
Mudge & Yarwood Co., Whitby, ON 1873
New Dominion Organ Co., Saint John, NB 1875

New Dominion Organ Co., Woodstock, ON 1876
William Norris, North York, ON 1867
Oakes Organ Co., Clinton, ON 1889–91
Ontario Organ Co., Toronto, ON 1884
Peters Organs, St John's, NF ?
Polton and Baldwin Co., Winnipeg, MB 1887
Principal Pipe Organ Co., Woodstock, ON 1962–
Providence Organ Inc., Laval, QC 1946–
J. Rainer Co., Guelph, ON 1875
Rappe & Co., Kingston, ON 1871–87
John Reed (Acadia Organ Co.) ?
J. Reyner, Kingston, ON 1871–85
St. Joseph Organ Co., St. Joseph, ON c. 1905
Sabathil & Sons (harpsichords), Vancouver, BC 1958–
J. Slown, Owen Sound, ON 1871-89
D. & C. Smith & Brome Co., Quebec City, QC 1875
Smith & Scribner, Chatham, ON 1864–5
Frank Stevenson, North York, ON 1867
James Thornton & Co., Hamilton, ON 1871–89
Toronto Organ Co., Toronto, ON 1880
William Townsend, Toronto, ON 1848
Warren & Son Organ Co., Woodstock, ON 1907–22
J.G. Webb & Sons, Woodstock, ON 1914
Elijah West, West Farnham, QC 1860–75
T.W. White & Co., Hamilton, ON 1869
Willis & Baker, London, ON 1868
M.R. Willits & Assoc., Woodstock, ON 1962–72
Wilson & Co., Sherbrooke, QC ?
Wood, Powell & Co., Guelph, ON 1883
Woodstock Organ Co. – see Karn story.
Woodstock Pipe Organ Builders – see Karn story.

♪

Figure 123. The earliest organ ad run by Eaton's, printed in its fall/winter catalogue of 1902–03, p.176. Tens of thousands of such instruments were sold by mail order in this way. By 1904, however, the Goderich name disappeared as Eaton's bought the right to have its own name appear on the instruments it sold.

Figure 124. 1876 Dominion Organ Company ad (see account in the piano section under Dominion Organ & Piano Company). This illustration is typical of many ornate organ stylings, 1870–1910. Apart from the pump and bellows arrangement, the mechanics of the instrument were compacted into a space of 10 – 12 inches high, running the length of the keyboard. Everything above the reed-stop pulls was just furniture.

Figure 125. From a daguerreotype submitted for patent on 1 May 1874. The photograph is one of four in which Frederich Mudge (Mudge & Yarwood Co., Whitby, Ontario) applied for industrial-design protection. With registration number 117 being assigned, this appears to be the earliest keyboard patent issued under the Trade Mark and Design Act of 1868.

Figure 126. Portrait of Joseph Casavant, one of Quebec's most noted pipe-organ manufacturers, c. 1840.

Figure 127. Drawing from the Historical Atlas of Oxford County, p. 82.

Figure 128. 1921 staff photo of the Warren & Son Organ Co., Woodstock, Ontario. In the second row from the bottom (far left) is Charles Warren, company president, and to his left, Harry Karn, a son of Dennis Karn. (See also D.W. Karn & Company.)

CHAPTER ELEVEN

The Final Chord

The Sherlock-Manning factory on East St in Clinton had hummed with activity since it was built in 1898. When I had the opportunity to walk alone through the old derelict some ninety years later, just a few days before the final sale closed this last piano factory in Canada, nostalgic momentos of once great days literally jumped off the walls.

Copies of the *Colourful Wild West Weekly Comics* from 1910 were varnished to a wooden beam. Boxing reports and baseball schedules from the 1930s were still plastered above workbenches. Scores of initials and relatively "clean" graffiti were inscribed on the tongue-and-groove boards lining the toilet stalls. A forgotten souvenir that made me both laugh and cry was something fastened to the 14-foot-high ceiling of the finishing room.

It seems that a tradition had developed of nailing up a worker's varnish-caked boots on the day he retired or left the company. High overhead, beside each pair, in fine-lined black paint, was a brief eulogy to each man. "Curly Millhouser, died March 31, 1954." "Benno Dunbar, departed March 1, 1956." And beside the last crusty, exhibit of shiny black leather were the words "Charlie Houghton, last seen heading toward Windsor in a black Studebaker sedan, looking for more money and women."

Such relics of a once thriving industry have diminished with each passing decade – forgotten by new and different generations.

The year 1991 marks the 175th anniversary of piano building in Canada. Since the modest efforts of German immigrant Friedrich Hund in a small Quebec City shop in 1816, more than 240 different manufacturers and principal "name" pianos have appeared in this country.

Some of these businesses were small, private workshops. Some were corporations employing hundreds of people. Many of Canada's piano makers, as early newcomers to this land, arrived with generations of talent and inventiveness compressed in their genes. Scores of them showed a zeal for hard work, business integrity, and a desire to create instruments that have filled our homes with warmth and song.

Our piano builders have made towns thrive, cities proud. With quality instruments finding homes in virtually every corner of the world Canadian pianos and organs earned a reputation for excellence unsurpassed by anything else that has ever left our shores.

Yes, thousands of children have moaned over the orders to practice, sighed about the annual recital, or spurned parental commands to perform Chopin for visiting relatives. But still countless others have gone on to become fine musicians, providing entertainment for tens of millions, and owing it all to their early discipline with a piano.

The Canadian piano industry has been filled with adventurous men. Businessmen who were not afraid to take chances or risk entire fortunes. Men whose innovations, ideas, and designs *did* make a difference. Men who travelled far and wide by train, on clipper ship, with horse and wagon, to peddle the latest company wares to the willing and eager. Men who were labourers. And brave men who had to face their families with the heart-breaking news that their line of work, their product, their industry, was no longer wanted.

As author Clifford Ford suggests, "The invention of the phonograph [made] serious inroads into the music market place, changing the

Figure 129. London Phonograph Company, c. 1917, from the Hines Photographic Collection, London, Ontario. Writer Allan Noon further describes this photo in his 1988 book **East of Adelaide** *as a right-hand drive McLaughlin Buick carrying an advertisement for Rayola Silver-Tone Phonographs. The driver/salesman called on homes in working-class neighbourhoods selling phonographs and records on easy credit terms.*

DOWNRIGHT UPRIGHT 137

habits of Canadians. Production and sale of pianos, in particular, were dependent upon the demand from a large body of amateur musicians. The coming of the player piano, followed by the phonograph, provided the musically illiterate the same satisfaction from musical entertainment in the home. This caused a decrease in active and an increase in passive music making."1`

The reasons for the death of the piano business are clearly seen as we look back. But at the time, as each company closed its doors and as the auction gavel silenced factories, these reasons were not as obvious. Disappointment and frustration were abundant.

It wasn't any one thing that caused the downfall of this once proud and powerful industry. It wasn't the phonograph or the radio, the automobile, or the television. It was all of them. What had once been the centre of entertainment in the home, the item around which entire families lovingly gathered, was slowly replaced by other pastimes. Entertainment was now available at the turn of a crank, a knob, or a key. By the mid-1920s many used cars were in the same price range as a new piano. If the average family had the choice, which would they choose? Which would you have chosen?

But the memory of such days is still alive. It echoes across this nation – indeed across the entire world – every time the keys of a Canadian-made piano are depressed. And the music lives on in the hearts of all who have loved the versatility, power, and expressiveness of a well-played piano.

So many of us have found deep satisfaction and joy in the products made by this extraordinary Canadian industry. So many have found the piano to be a lifelong friend.

As the sound of the final chord slowly fades away, I wonder if Charlie Houghton, whose boots were spiked to that ceiling in Clinton, ever found what he was looking for. ♪

GIANTS OF THE KEYBOARD
(PUBLISHER'S INSERT)

Norm Amadio

Canada may no longer be producing pianos, but our pianists are among the best in the world. Brief sketches of a few of the exceptional, feature some early moments and experiences with pianos.

"He can play with anybody, anywhere."
– *Henry Cuesta speaking of Norm Amadio*

The Northern Ontario mining community of Timmins is the birthplace of a true legend in Canadian music, Norm Amadio. Within Toronto Jazz circles it is widely believed that the genial Amadio is the most complete piano player around. Famed clarinetist, Henry Cuesta, once summed up his professional regard for Norm Amadio by publicly stating, "He's a giant, that's all. He can play with anybody, anywhere."

Both Norm and his bass player brother, John, were musically influenced by their father, John Sr., who played the mandolin with a Timmins band and occasionally "tinkled the ivories". Norm recalls that his Dad purchased a used Willis player piano in 1933. It wasn't until 1936, at his Mother's insistence, that the young Amadio commenced twice weekly piano lessons and began to practice for an hour every morning before he went to school. His music teachers were the Gray sisters at Holy Family School and each lesson cost the Amadio household 50¢.

Rather than take work in the mines, Norm acted on his Mother's suggestion to leave Timmins for Toronto and to study piano under Boris Berlin at the Royal Conservatory of Music. The year was 1946. Following ten months of intense study, Amadio realized that his musical ambitions lay in the areas outside of classical music. He began to frequent Toronto's after hours jazz clubs and sit in on jam sessions at the old Mercury Club on Victoria Street. In no time, Norm was the talk of Toronto jazz circles and he soon found himself playing with such famous musicians as Lester Young, Stan Getz, Dizzy Gillespie and singer Billie Holiday. When speaking of his own musical roots back in Timmins, Amadio has often said that "Jazz can come from anywhere as long as you have the feel for it." To which could be added that a great left hand, a marvellous disposition and a gigantic constitution, all of which he possesses, are assets any up and coming piano player would envy.

GIANTS OF THE KEYBOARD

(PUBLISHER'S INSERT)

John Arpin

"There's history in his fingers."
– Peter Goddard, Toronto Star

Pianist, composer, arranger, John Arpin has long been regarded as one of the most versatile performers on the Canadian music scene. Born in Port McNicoll, Ontario, many older hometown residents still remember his father's little confectionery store - complete with juke box, and young John's piano practice emanating from the Arpin living quarters behind the store.

John Arpin's first piano was the one that his mother purchased as a young single woman. She had saved her nickels and dimes while working as a seamstress for Hobberlin's in Toronto. She bought the upright piano from Heintzman's - however, it bore the stamp of The Canada Piano Company. The instrument remained with her after she married, and at age four, John and his brother, Leo, took their lessons on that same piano. The story of the Arpin family piano regrettably came to an unfortunate end. Following his mother's death in 1975, John arranged with a flea market dealer in Victoria Harbour for the storage of the piano and other family possessions. The dealer was paid $500.00 for moving the items and for an agreed upon period of storage. A few weeks later, John and his son returned to Victoria Harbour in order to begin moving things back to Toronto. To their dismay they found the storage place "cleaner than a whistle," and following local enquiries discovered that the departed dealer had sold everything at auction.

John Arpin graduated from the Royal Conservatory of Music at the age of sixteen. Following a year at the Faculty of Music, University of Toronto, he became an active member of the local music scene and for many years, both as a soloist and as a leader of his own trio, played in Toronto's leading night clubs.

Arpin's many recordings and his live concerts in Canada and the U.S.A., have earned the affable Canadian a sizeable following. Possessing diverse musical abilities, he also composes, arranges and conducts. Though he plays everything from the classics to film and stage songs, John Arpin's name has become synonymous with piano rags. He is generally acknowledged as one of the top two or three ragtime musicians in the world. No less a musician than the late Eubie

Blake pronounced him "The Chopin of Ragtime", while the New York Times labelled him "The Richter of Ragtime".

At presstime, John Arpin personally provided the publisher of *Downright Upright* with the following story:

"Years ago, when I was a teenager and had only recently arrived in Toronto, I had the good fortune of meeting a young gentleman, Basil McCormick. Basil became a close musical friend. Through him, I got to know some of the people who worked at the old Heintzman building on Yonge Street. One of these people was a chap called Ruben, somewhere in his sixties. He was the night elevator operator and watchman for the building after closing hours. It was only a matter of time till I discovered the famed Artist Room on the fourth floor. This room contained two wonderful Heintzman concert-grand pianos. They were placed in the center of the room, dovetailed. What magnificent pianos they were, always tuned and well maintained. My brain began to work overtime and I suggested to Ruben that perhaps I could practice now and again. He told me that I could come over any time during the night when he was working, but to be discreet and not mention anything about this to anyone associated with Heintzman's. There began a three times a week all night practice vigil in the Artist Room at Heintzman's store playing on two super pianos. Ruben would listen, make his rounds, come back and listen again and also show great interest by making positive comments about how I was progressing. I'll always be indebted to him, even though I never got to know his last name or where he lived."

GIANTS OF THE KEYBOARD

(PUBLISHER'S INSERT)

Glenn Gould

Glenn Gould grew up surrounded by numerous musical family influences not the least of whom was his grandmother, who for many years, performed in the Uxbridge Businessmen's Bible Class Orchestra. A pianist, grandmother had an early Uxbridge-made piano, which she played up until her death in her 90th year. Glenn's own lessons commenced at age three and he first played on his mother's Heintzman upright.

Father, Russell "Bert" Gould, played violin in the local orchestra and recalled for *Downright Upright* Publisher, Barry Penhale, the devastating fire of the old Uxbridge Piano and Organ Company, in the early 1900's. He also remembered George McGuire, a principal in the Uxbridge Piano and Organ Company, a clarinet player and local band leader of note.

Glenn's Dad, would trailer upright pianos up to the family cottage at Lake Simcoe, which Bert built in 1933. Through the years the Gould's took five or six uprights to the cottage, among them an upright Heintzman grand, a Bell, and an instrument produced by the Dominion Piano Company. Later in a special addition to the cottage, Glenn would play on two concert grands.

Several pianos from the Gould family cottage came back to Toronto to see use in Glenn's school - Williamson Road Public School. When on occasion the pianos wintered at Lake Simcoe, a light cord with bulb positioned close to the strings was placed inside the instrument and the lid kept closed.

The cottage environment throughout the years was to have a profound effect on a remarkable Canadian destined to become one of the truly great musicians of the 20th century. While he went on to become internationally acclaimed as a pianist of prodigious talent, Gould proved equally remarkable as a composer, recording artist, CBC radio documentary writer/producer and in his last year had begun to work as a recording conductor.

When Glenn Gould announced in 1964, at age 32, his decision to give up live concerts, many friends and colleagues feared he would lose his eminence in the international music world. With extraordinary foresight, however, he consolidated his career as a recording artist with CBS Records. He influenced a new generation of performers and listeners through his illuminating interpretations of the music of a variety of composers, and in particular, of Bach. His probing and sometimes controversial explorations of his extensive musical repertoire resulted in intensely personal re-creations of classical works, which became milestones in the evolution of musical interpretation and performance.

Glenn Gould's passion for using media technologies to communicate his ideas began at the outset of his long association with the Canadian Broadcasting Corporation. In addition to his numerous performances on radio, Gould broke new artistic ground with his documentaries on radio and his television essays and performances. Now republished, his writings reveal a profound musical insight and are stimulating interest among new audiences.

Glenn Gould's untimely death on 4 October 1982, just several days after his fiftieth birthday, was mourned by music lovers everywhere. Through his recordings and other contributions to the mass media, Glenn Gould has left a rich legacy of musical ideas and performances which continue to challenge and inspire new generations throughout the world.

THE GLENN GOULD PRIZE

The Glenn Gould Prize is an international prize, which was awarded for the first time in November 1987. It was created by the Glenn Gould Foundation, and is intended as a tribute by the people of Canada to the life and work of Glenn Gould. The Prize, which will be awarded every three years, consists of $50,000 and a work of art by a Canadian artist.

The Glenn Gould Prize is intended to recognize an exceptional contribution to music and its communication, through the use of any communications technologies.

The prize is administered by the Canada Council, an organization which provides grants and services to artists and arts organizations.

Glenn Gould with grandmother Grieg.

Glenn Gould with pet dog "Ricky."

GIANTS OF THE KEYBOARD

(PUBLISHER'S INSERT)

Anton Kuerti

"There is no doubt that pianist Anton Kuerti is a national treasure."
– Gillian Haggart, London Free Press

Though an acclaimed international performer, Anton Kuerti's popularity throughout his adopted Canada is such that one wonders how the Vienna-born classical pianist finds the time and energy to go abroad. Altogether he has given concerts in more than 100 Canadian cities, ranging from Victoria, BC to St. John's, Newfoundland. In addition to recitals and chamber music performances from coast to coast, Kuerti is heard regularly on CBC Radio and Television not only as a pianist, but also as a commentator, conductor and composer.

In 1980 Anton Kuerti was instrumental in founding the "Festival of the Sound", in Parry Sound, Ontario, now considered one of Canada's most significant summer music festivals. There he enjoys performing chamber music, another of his special musical interests. It would be hard to find an important piece of piano chamber music that he has not performed with partners like Shmuel Ashkenasi, Toshiya Eto, Sidney Harth, Mark Kaplan, Yo-Yo Ma, Joseph Silverstein, Janos Starker, Walter Trampler, Barry Tuckwell, and the Cleveland, Guarneri, Orford, Tokyo and Vermeer string quartets.

Kuerti takes a special interest in the piano mechanism, and is considered to be almost unique among pianists as a technician of the highest qualifications. It is not unusual to find him regulating and voicing a piano just hours before a concert. Often he takes one of his own concert pianos on tour with him in his own specially modified van.

In addition to the enjoyment of his contrasting Toronto and Georgian Bay lifestyles, Anton Kuerti has many interests outside music, including hiking, sailing, skiing, science, literature and politics. He has been a vegetarian most of his life, and is an active supporter of the peace movement, frequently giving benefit concerts for organizations like Amnesty International and Oxfam.

If there is any characterization of Kuerti's art which seems to recur in reviews all over the world, it is his "very individual ideas" (*New York Times*). "Anton Kuerti is a pianist like Hoffman, Paderewski and the great individualists of the early 20th century" (*Vancouver Sun*). "Anton Kuerti is and remains a 'special' pianist, one who never leaves you indifferent and whom you will remember long after having left the concert hall" (*Le Soleil*, Quebec). Perhaps the Boston *Globe* said it best in reference to Anton Kuerti's stature as a pianist "of as great distinction as one is likely to encounter."

"It is truly a pity that the Heintzman piano is no longer being manufactured. Thereby one more worthy bit of Canadiana is extinguished. Heintzman was a product that Canada can be justly proud of; the best Heintzmans are exquisite instruments indeed, with a very individual, characteristic tone that is bright without becoming metallic or distorted. While I have not often played Heintzmans in concert – and have seen only a very few concert grands – I have frequently enjoyed practising on them. I think it is not unfair to contend that Heintzman ranks among the top 10 pianos built in this century."

– *Anton Kuerti*

Anton Kuerti, with Econoline van transporting piano 1976.

GIANTS OF THE KEYBOARD
(PUBLISHER'S INSERT)

Oscar Peterson

"Most piano players end when he starts."
– *Gene Lees, author, lyricist, music critic*

It's difficult to know just where to begin, when describing the career and accomplishments of Montreal-born Oscar Peterson. Canada's best-known jazz pianist has garnered ten honourary degrees, three different Hall of Fame awards, assorted music awards including the Playboy Award "Best Jazz Pianist," twelve times; Downbeat Award "Best Jazz Pianist," thirteen times; Contemporary Keyboard Award "Best Jazz Pianist," five times and at last count, six grammies. As if these important awards haven't already contributed to a packed trophy room. Peterson has also received some thirty other major awards including the Order of Canada as an Officer and the Order of Canada as a Companion.

Oscar Peterson's parents were immigrants to Canada from the British West Indies and the Virgin Islands. His father, Daniel Peterson, whose occupation was boswain on a sailing vessel, met his mother, Olivia John at the time, in Montreal where she had landed as a cook and housekeeper for an English family. They decided to remain in Canada, get married and start a family, which they did.

Oscar was the fourth of five children in the Peterson household, and their father wasted no time in starting each member of the Peterson clan on piano. They were later farmed out to various teachers when they surpassed father Peterson's teaching capabilities.

Oscar Peterson studied with the gifted Hungarian classical pianist, Paul deMarky, and a warm and respectful musical and personal friendship developed between the two.

During this period, Peterson won the Ken Soble Amateur Show and made various appearances on local radio shows as guest artist and appeared on national radio shows such as the Happy Gang, and the Light Up and Listen Hour.

Shortly after this period, he was signed up by RCA Victor Records and made varied tours across Canada playing concerts. At the same point in time, Peterson did a stint in the Johnny Holmes Orchestra as the featured pianist.

In 1947 Peterson formed his first Canadian trio and retained this format of performance for the next couple of years. During this time he remained dedicated to establishing a true trio sound. It was during one of these appearances that impresario Norman Granz heard him and enticed him into making an appearance with his all-star concert troupe known as "Jazz at the Philharmonic." After a successful Carnegie Hall debut in 1949, Peterson returned home for a year, and rejoined the group as a steady member in 1950. He then commenced recording for Norman Granz under his Verve record label and formed his first U.S. duo with bassist Ray Brown.

Over the years, Oscar Peterson has recorded with most of the jazz greats including Louis Armstrong, Ella Fitzgerald, Count Basie, Duke Ellington and Dizzy Gillespie. In recent times, however, Peterson has chosen to devote more and more time to composition. By limiting most of his recent live performances to concerts with the Oscar Peterson Trio and some occasional nightclub work, he has freed up valuable time for composition and the countless commissions that continually come his way.

Oscar Peterson resides in the City of Mississauga. As a citizen he insists on his privacy which he jealously guards. When not at home, he immediately escapes to the Haliburton Highlands of Ontario where he has a cottage. He is a devotee of fly fishing and enjoys endless hours of this placid sport. His hobbies include photography, astronomy, and he is an avid audiophile and synthesist. His home contains his own private recording studio which houses varied instruments and a host of high technology recording equipment. Peterson became interested in the technological end of the recording industry due to the many hours spent in recording studios. He retains a workable knowledge of all of the electronic and computerized equipment that abounds in his home.

An adjunct Professor of Music in Jazz Studies at York University since 1986, Oscar Peterson has recently become the eighth Chancellor of this important suburban Toronto university.

Both at home and abroad, Peterson continues to dominate as the world's supreme jazz pianist. He is also unequalled as Canada's foremost ambassador of goodwill, as a result of his many popular tours of the United States, Europe, Africa, South America, the Far East and Russia.

♪

NOTES

INTRODUCTION
1 Eric Partridge, *A Dictionary of Slang and Unconventional English*, 8th edition, Paul Beale, ed. (Routledge and Kegan Paul, London, 1984).
2 Eric Partridge, *A Dictionary of the Underworld* (Routledge and Kegan Paul, London, 1949).
3 Eric Partridge, *A Dictionary of Slang and Unconventional English*.
4 Clarence Major, *A Dictionary of Afro-American Slang* (International Publishers Co., New York, 1970).
5 *A Dictionary of Americanisms on Historical Priciples*, Mitford M. Matthews, ed. (University of Chicago Press, Chicago, 1951).

CHAPTER ONE
1 Murray Draper, *W.D. – The Story of Doherty and Sherlock-Manning* (Clinton Commercial Printers, 1986), p.27.
2 *Commercial and Industrial Edition of Port Hope, Bowmanville, Orono and Newcastle, Ontario* (1916).
3 Clifford Ford, *Canada's Music: An Historical Survey* (GLC Publishers Ltd., Agincourt, ON, 1982).
4 James McCook, "Some Notes on Musical Instruments Among the Pioneers of the Canadian West," *Canadian Music Journal*, vol. II, (Winter 1958), p.23.
5 McKenzie Porter, "The Piano with the All-Canadian Tone," *Maclean's*, 11 May 1957, p.34.
6 Allan McGillivray, notes from the Uxbridge-Scott Historical Society (unpublished).
7 Craig Roell, *The Piano in America, 1890–1940*, (University of North Carolina Press, Chapel Hill, NC, 1989), p.xii.

CHAPTER TWO
1 Willy Amtmann, *Music in Canada: 1600–1800* (Collier-Macmillan Canada Ltd., 1975), p.112.
2 *Ibid.*, pp.209 – 10.
3 Quebec *Gazette*, 10 June 1788.
4 Montreal *Gazette*, 3 September 1789.
5 Timothy McGee, *The Music of Canada* (Penguin Books Canada Ltd., Markham, ON, 1985), p.35.
6 *Ibid.*, p.53.
7 Helmut Kallmann et al, eds., *Encyclopedia of Music in Canada* (hereafter EMC)(University of Toronto Press, Toronto, 1981), pp.752 – 55.
8 Ernest Closson, *History of the Piano* (Elek Books Ltd. London, 1944), p.101.
9 Helmut Kallmann, *A History of Music in Canada: 1534–1914* (University of Toronto Press, Toronto, 1960), p.160.
10 James McCook, *The Canadian Music Journal*, Winter 1958, p.22.
11 *Ibid.*, p.23.
12 Helmut Kallmann, *A History of Music in Canada*, p.167.
13 *Ibid.*, p.161 – 62.
14 Clifford Ford, *Canada's Music*, p.2.
15 *Ibid.*, p.3.

CHAPTER THREE
1 W.L. Sumner *The Pianoforte* (Macdonald & Co.,

London, England, 1966), p.66.
2 Ernest Closson, *History of the Piano*, p.148.
3 *Ibid.*, p.101.
4 *Waterloo Historical Society Reports*, vol. 4 (1928–32), p.179.
5 *Semi-Weekly Spectator*, Hamilton, ON, 11 September 1858.
6 Cyril Ehrlich, *The Piano: A History* (J.M. Dent & Sons, London, England, 1976), p.140.
7 Murray Draper, *W.D. – The Story of Doherty and Sherlock-Manning*, pp.15 – 16.

CHAPTER FOUR
1 Alfred Dolge, *Pianos and Their Makers* (Covina Publishing Company, Covina, CA, 1972, reprint of 1911), p.84.

CHAPTER FIVE
1 Ross Skoggard, *The London Free Press*, 12 August 1986.
2 *Globe*, Toronto, 19 July 1912.
3 *Sherlock-Manning Piano Company*, 1921 brochure, p.12.
4 *EMC*, p.765.

CHAPTER SIX
1 Donald E. Coulman, *Guelph: Take a Look at Us Now*, (Boston Mills Press, Erin, ON, 1977).
2 Leo A. Johnson, *History of Guelph: 1827–1927* (Guelph Historical Society, 1977).
3 *Globe*, 3 August 1889.
4 *Guelph Herald* (illustrated edition, December 1895), p.5.
5 *Historical Atlas of Wellington County*, 1906, p.14.
6 *Ibid.*, p.15.
7 W.J. Bell, *Municipal Ownership and Civic Government by Commission* (Guelph Board of Trade, 1909 edition), p.23.
8 *Clinton New Era*, 19 January 1900.
9 *The Farmer's Advocate*, London, ON, October 1906, p.2,011.
10 Jabez Rands, *Histories of Huron County* (unpublished, 1974).
11 *Commercial and Industrial Edition of Port Hope, Bowmanville, Orono and Newcastle, Ontario* (1916).
12 *Canadian Statesman*, Bowmanville, ON, 13 December 1905, p.1.
13 *The Dominion Organ and Piano Co. Ltd. Brochure*, c. 1910, p.3.
14 Daniel Hoffman, "The Dominion Organ & Piano Co.Revisited," *Belvedere* (journal of the Bowmanville Museum), Summer 1988, p.13.
15 *Sentinel Review*, Woodstock, ON, 12 May 1899.
16 *Ingersoll Sun*, 12 February 1907.
17 *Toronto Mail*, 28 May 1892, p.12.
18 *Ingersoll Times*, 2 December 1981, p.11.
19 *Industrial Ingersoll Illustrated*, 10 February 1907.
20 Edna M. Meek, personal communication, 6 December 1988.
21 *Hamilton, The Electric City* (City of Hamilton, 1906), p.29.
22 *EMC*, p.423.
23 McKenzie Porter, "The Piano with the All-Canadian Tone," *Maclean's*, 11 May 1957, p.36.
24 *Ibid.*, p.37.
25 *Woodstock Express Industrial Number*, February 1906, p.14.
26 *Sentinel Review*, 1 July 1901, p.4.
27 *Ibid.*, 3 September 1974.
28 *Lesage Pianos Ltd. Brochure*, c. 1970; Histoire de Ste Thérèse-de-Blainville: 1787–1939 (Societe Historique de Ste Thérèse, 1940, pp.234 – 49.
29 *EMC*, p.541.
30 Jacques Roy, *Gazette*, Montreal, 1 May 1982, p.E2.
31 Jean Bertrand, "Pianos Lesage Manace de Fermeture," *La Voiz des Milles-Iles*, 3 April 1986.
32 *EMC*, p.602.
33 *Listowel Banner*, 1 April 1892.
34 *Centennial at Listowel* (Listowel Centennial Committee, 1975), p.18.
35 *Listowel Banner*, 20 March 1924.
36 *Globe*, 2 July 1904, p.27.
37 *EMC*, p.675.
38 *Globe*, 2 July 1904, p.44.
39 *Hamilton Times*, 20 April 1907.
40 *EMC*, pp.680 – 81.
41 *Globe*, 31 July 1912, p.8.
42 *London Free Press*, 10 January 1925.
43 Murray Draper, *W.D. – The Story of Doherty and Sherlock-Manning*, p.42.
44 Jay Teitel, "Piano Forte," *Quest*, May 1982, p.42.
45 *Huron Historical Notes*, vol.24 (1988), p.25.

46 There is an astonishing lack of information concerning this significant part of Kingston's past. Neither Kingston Public Library nor the archives at Queen's University were able to provide details on the local piano trade. One single page of sketchy information was gleaned from the two sources. Local newspapers have not been indexed prior to 1950, limiting the search further. Again, as noted previously, it appears that the piano industry in this city – as elsewhere – was taken for granted for many years, viewed as frivolous and not considered worthy of documentation.
47 *Kingston City Directories*, 1860–1900.
48 *EMC*, p.1,002.
49 T.E. Kaiser, *Historical Sketches of Oshawa* (The Reformer Printing & Publishing Co. Ltd., 1921), p.167.
50 M. McIntyre Hood, *Oshawa, the Crossing Between the Waters: A History of Canada's Motor City* (McLaughlin Public Library, 1968), pp.78 – 79.
51 John James Willis, *Reminiscences of the Family Business* (unpublished), c. 1950.

CHAPTER SEVEN
1 Matt Willis, personal communication, 3 March 1989.
2 *Amherst Daily News*, 22 February 1918.
3 Norma Joan Paul, *Pastimes*, Oct./Nov. 1981, p.4.
4 G.A. White, publisher, *Halifax and Its Business* (1876), p.96.
5 *EMC*, p.27.
6 Robert Dale McIntosh, *A Documentary History of Music in Victoria, British Columbia*, vol.I: 1850–99 (University of Victoria, Victoria, BC, 1981), p.106.
7 *British Colonist*, Victoria, BC, 15 June 1881, p.3.
8 Patent Office, Ottawa, assorted materials, March 1989.
9 *Berlin News Record*, 14 April 1900, p.1.
10 *Berlin: A Self-Portrait of Kitchener Before World War I*, (City of Kitchener) p.16.
11 Patent Office, Ottawa, assorted materials, March 1989.
12 *Recorder*, Halifax, 19 September 1870, p.2.
13 *Halifax and Its Business*, p.96.
14 *London Free Press*, 11 September 1906, p.6; *Canadian Music Trades Journal*, January 1901.
15 *Eaton's Fall and Winter Catalogue*, 1909–10, p.151.
16 *Greater Vancouver City Directory for 1938*, p.1,905.
17 *Hamilton Times*, 17 October 1905, p.1.
18 *British Colonist*, 15 June 1881, p.4.
19 Robert Dale McIntosh, *A Documentary History of Music in Victoria* vol. 1, p.141.
20 *EMC*, p.388.
21 William Weld, *The Farmer's Advocate*, October 1906, p.1,640.
22 "Music House in 20th Year," *Border Cities Star*, Windsor, 7 October 1927, p.7.
23 *EMC*, p.426.
24 *Guelph Herald*, December 1895, p.5.
25 *Semi-Weekly Spectator*, 11 September 1858.
26 *The Gerhard Heintzman 1894 Catalogue*, p.2.
27 *EMC*, p.716.
28 *Ibid.*, p.611.
29 *Ibid.*, p.621.
30 Murray Draper, *W.D. – The Story of Doherty and Sherlock-Manning*, p.48.
31 Benjamin S. Scott, *The Economic and Industrial History of the City of London, 1855–1930* (self-published thesis, October 1930), p.187.
32 Dan Hoffman, *Belvedere*, Winter 1987, p.12.
33 Allan McGillivray, notes from the Uxbridge-Scott Historical Society (unpublished).
34 *Halifax and Its Business*, p.97.
35 *EMC*, p.772.
36 *Ibid.*, p.790; Histoire de Ste Thérèse-de-Blainville, 1787–1939, pp.234 – 49.
37 Murray Draper, *W.D. – The Story of Doherty and Sherlock-Manning*, p.23.
38 *EMC*, p.621.
39 Patent Office, Ottawa, assorted materials, March 1989.
40 *Ingersoll Times*, 2 December 1981, p.11.
41 *Ingersoll Sun*, February 1907.
42 George MacLean, ed. *A Cyclopedia of Canadian Biography: Being Chiefly Men of the Time* (Toronto, 1886).
43 *Hamilton Herald*, 5 October 1891, p.1.
44 *Sentinel Review*, 1 July 1910, p.4.
45 Allan McGillivray, *Uxbridge-Scott Historical Society Notes*, unpublished.
46 *Sentinel Review*, 1 July 1901, p.4.
47 *Waterloo Historical Society Reports*, vol. 56

(1968–72), p.84.
48 Canadian sheet music stacks, Metropolitan Toronto Reference Library.
49 *Halifax and Its Business*, p.98.
50 *City of London Directory*, 1877–78, p.78.
51 *Strathroy Centennial: 1860–1960* (Strathroy Centennial Committee, 1960), pp.36 – 37.

CHAPTER EIGHT
1 Bob Pierce, *Pierce Piano Atlas*, 8th edition (copyright Bob Pierce, Long Beach, CA, 1982).
2 Bob Pierce, personal communication, 22 October 1988.

CHAPTER NINE
1 Edwin M. Good, *Giraffes, Black Dragons and Other Pianos* (Stanford University Press, Stanford, CN, 1982), p.5.

CHAPTER TEN
1 Benjamin S. Scott, *The Economic and Industrial History of the City of London, 1855–1930*, p.189.

CHAPTER ELEVEN
1 Clifford Ford, *Canada's Music: An Historical Survey*, p.60.

BIBLIOGRAPHY

Amherst Daily News, 22 February 1918.
Amtmann, Willy. *Music in Canada: 1600–1800*. Habitex Books, distributed by Collier-Macmillan Canada Ltd. Cambridge, ON, 1975.
Bell, W.J. *Municipal Ownership and Civic Government by Commission*. Guelph Board of Trade, 1909 edition.
Berlin: A Self-Portrait of Kitchener Before World War I City of Kitchener, 1946.
Berlin News Record, 14 April 1900.
Bertrand, Jean. "Pianos Lesage Menace de Fermeture," *La Voix des Milles-Iles*, 3 April 1986.
Border Cities Star, Windsor, 7 October 1927.
British Colonist, Victoria, 15 June 1881.
Ibid., 4 March 1890.
Canadian Music Trades Journal, 1900–1930.
Canadian sheet music stacks, Metropolitan Toronto Reference Library.
Canadian Statesman, Bowmanville, ON, 13 December 1905.
Centennial At Listowel. Listowel Centennial Committee, 1975.
Clinton New Era, 19 January 1900.

Closson, Ernest. *History of the Piano*. Elek Books Ltd. London, 1944.
Commercial and Industrial Edition of Port Hope, Bowmanville, Orono and Newcastle, Ontario. 1916.
Coulman, Donald E. *Guelph: Take a Look at Us Now*, Boston Mills Press. Erin, ON, 1977.
Dolge, Alfred. *Pianos and Their Makers*. Covina Publishing, Covina, CA, 1972 (reprint of 1911).
The Dominion Organ and Piano Co. Ltd. Brochure, c. 1910.
Dorrington, Aubrey, *History of Stellarton*, Advocate Printing & Publishing Co., 1976.
Draper, Murray. W.D. – *The story of Doherty & Sherlock-Manning*. Clinton Commercial Printers, Clinton, ON, 1986.
Eaton's Fall & Winter Catalogue, 1909–10.
Ehrlich, Cyril. *The Piano: A History*. J.M. Dent & Sons, London, 1976.
Evans, Anne. personal communication, 11 October 1989.
Farmer's Advocate and Home Magazine, William Weld, publisher, October 1906.
Fine, Larry. *The Piano Book, A Guide to Buying a New or*

Used Piano. Brookside Press, Boston, MA, 1987.

Finlayson, Ann. "They Shoot Piano-Makers Don't They?" *Maclean's*, 3 November 1980.

Ford, Clifford. *Canada's Music: An Historical Survey*. GLC Publishers Ltd., Agincourt, ON, 1982.

Gaines, James R., ed. *The Lives of the Piano*. Holt, Rinehart, Winston, New York, 1981.

Gazette, Sarnia, 16 April 1911.

The Gerhard Heintzman 1894 Catalogue.

Gill, Dominic, ed. *The Book of the Piano*. Phaidon Press Ltd., Oxford, England, 1981.

Gillespie, John. *Five Centuries of Keyboard Music*. Wadsworth Publishing Co. Inc., Belmont, CA, 1965.

Globe, Toronto, 3 August 1889, 2 July 1904, 19 and 31 July 1912.

Good, Edwin M. *Giraffes, Black Dragons and Other Pianos*. Stanford University Press, Stanford, CN, 1982.

Gould, Susan; Fredericks, Robert. *The Official Price Guide to Music Collectibles*. (1st edition). House of Collectibles Inc., Orlando, FL, 1980.

The Greater Vancouver City Directory For 1938.

Grover, David S. *The Piano: Its Story from Zither to Grand*. Robert Hale Ltd., London, 1976.

Guelph Herald (Illustrated Edition), December 1895.

Hamilton, The Electric City. City of Hamilton, 1906.

Hamilton Herald, 5 October 1891.

Hamilton Times, 17 October 1905, 29 April 1907.

Harrison, Sidney. *Grand Pianos*. Faber and Faber, London, 1976.

Hipkins, Alfred J. *A Description and History of the Pianoforte* (3rd edition) Information Coordinators Incorporated, Detroit, MI, 1975.

Histoire de Ste Thérèse-de-Blainville: 1787–1939, Societe Historique de Sainte Thérèse, 1940.

Historical Atlas of Wellington County, 1906.

Hoffman, Dan. *Belvedere*, (journal of the Bowmanville Museum) winter 1987; summer 1988.

Hollis, Helen Rice. *The Piano: A Pictorial Account of Its Ancestry and Development*. Douglas David & Charles Ltd. London, 1975.

Hood, M. McIntyre. *Oshawa, The Crossing between the Waters: A History of Canada's Motor City*. McLaughlin Public Library, 1968.

Industrial Ingersoll Illustrated, 10 February 1907.

Ingersoll Sun, 12 February 1907

Ingersoll Times, 2 December 1981.

James, Philip. *Early Keyboard Instruments: From Their Beginning to the Year 1820*. Barnes & Noble, Inc., New York, 1970.

Johnson, Leo A. *History of Guelph: 1827–1927*. Guelph Historical Society, 1977.

Kaiser, T.E. *Historical Sketches of Oshawa*. The Reformer Printing and Publishing Co. Ltd., 1921.

Kallmann, Helmut. *A History of Music in Canada: 1534–1914* University of Toronto Press, Toronto, 1960.

Kallmann, Helmut and Beckwith, John. "Making of Musical Instruments," *Encyclopedia Canadiana*, vol. 7. Grolier of Canada, Toronto, 1977.

Kallmann, Helmut; Potvin, Gilles; Winters, Kenneth, eds. *Encyclopedia of Music in Canada*. University of Toronto Press, Toronto, 1981.

Kingston City Directories, 1860–1900.

Lesage Pianos Ltd. Product Brochure, c. 1970.

Listowel Banner, 1 April 1892; 20 March 1924.

London City Directory, 1877–78.

London Free Press, 11 September 1906; 22 January 1972

MacLean, George, ed. *A Cyclopedia of Canadian Biography: Being Chiefly Men of the Time*. Toronto, 1886.

McCombie, Ian. *The Piano Handbook*. Charles Scribner's Sons, New York, 1980.

McCook, James. "Some Notes on Musical Instruments among the Pioneers of the Canadian West", *The Canadian Music Journal*, vol. 2 (Winter 1958).

McIntosh, Robert Dale. *A Documentary History of Music in Victoria, British Columbia, vol. 1: 1850–1889*. University of Victoria, 1981.

McGee, Timothy J. *The Music of Canada*. Penguin Books Canada Ltd., Markham, ON, 1985.

McGillivray, Allan. *"Notes on the Uxbridge Piano and Organ Company,"* Uxbridge-Scott Historical Society. unpublished.

Meek, Edna M. personal communication, 6 December 1988.

Montreal Gazette, 3 September 1789.

Oringer, Judith, *Passion for the Piano*, Jeremy P. Tarcher, Inc., Los Angeles, CA, 1983.

Paul, Norma Joan, *Pastimes*, Oct./Nov. 1981.

Pierce, Bob. *Pierce Piano Atlas (7th edition)*. Copyright Bob Pierce, Long Beach, CA, 1965; (8th edition), 1982.

Porter, McKenzie. "The Piano with the All-Canadian Tone," *MacLean's*, 11 May 1957.

Rands, Jabez, *Histories of Huron County*, unpublished, 1974.

Ratcliffe, Ronald V. *Steinway*. Chronicle Books, San Francisco, CA, 1989.

Recorder, Halifax, 19 September 1870.

Roell, Craig H. *The Piano in America, 1890–1940*, University of North Carolina Press, Chapel Hill, NC, 1989.

Roy, Jacques, *Gazette*, Montreal, 1 May 1982.

Sadie, Stanley, ed. *The Piano*. W.W. Norton & Co., New York, 1988.

Schmeckel, Carl D. *The Piano Owner's Guide*. Charles Scribner's Sons, New York, 1974.

Scott, Benjamin S. *The Economic and Industrial History of City of London: 1855–1930*. Self-published thesis, October 1930.

Semi-Weekly Spectator, Hamilton, 11 September 1858.

Sentinel Review, Woodstock, ON, 12 May 1899; 1 July 1901; 3 September 1974.

Sherlock-Manning Piano Company, 1921 brochure.

Skoggard, Ross. *London Free Press*, 12 August 1986.

Strathroy Centennial. Strathroy Centennial Committee, 1960.

Sumner, W.L. *The Pianoforte*. Macdonald and Co. Ltd., London, 1966.

Teitel, Jay. "Piano Forte", *Quest*, magazine, May 1982.

Toronto Mail, 28 May 1892.

Toronto Star, 9 January 1988.

Walter, Arnold, ed. *Aspects of Music in Canada*. University of Toronto Press, Toronto, 1969.

Waterloo Historical Society Reports, vol. 4 (1928–32; vol. 56 (1968–72).

White, G.A. Publisher. *Halifax and Its Business*, 1876.

VISUALS CREDITS

Front Cover - Charles Heintzman;
Front Cover (inset) - Charles Heintzman;
Inside Front Cover - John Arpin;
Page 6 - John Arpin;

Fig. 1 - Ruth Kelly;
Fig. 2 - Tim Watcher;
Fig. 3 - Murray Draper;
Fig. 4 - Allan Noon;
Fig. 5 - London Public Library;
Fig. 6 - Murray Draper;
Fig. 7 - London Public Library;
Fig. 8 - ibid;
Fig. 9 - Huron County Museum, Goderich, Ontario;
Fig. 10 - Metropolitan Toronto Reference Library;
Fig. 11 - Huron County Museum, Goderich;
Fig. 12 - Smithsonian Institution, Photo #56-403A;
Fig. 13 - ibid., Photo #56-414A;
Fig. 14 - Douglas Barber, Patent Office, Ottawa;
Fig. 15 - ibid.;
Fig. 16 - ibid.;
Fig. 17 - ibid.;
Fig. 18 - ibid.;
Fig. 19 - ibid.;
Fig. 20 - ibid.;
Fig. 21 - Woodstock Public Library;
Fig. 22 - Metropolitan Toronto Reference Library;
Fig. 23 - Caleb Kelly;
Fig. 24 - Stewart Kelly;
Fig. 25 - London Public Library;
Fig. 26 - Metropolitan Toronto Reference Library;
Fig. 27 - ibid.;
Fig. 28 - ibid.;
Fig. 29 - author's collection;
Fig. 30 - author's photo;
Fig. 31 - ibid.;
Fig. 32 - Guelph Public Library;
Fig. 33 - Don Coulman;
Fig. 34 - London Public Library;
Fig. 35 - Guelph Public Library;
Fig. 36 - Murray Draper;
Fig. 37 - ibid.;

Fig. 38 - author's photo;
Fig. 39 - Murray Draper;
Fig. 40 - ibid.;
Fig. 41 - ibid.;
Fig. 42 - author's photo;
Fig. 43 - Bowmanville Museum;
Fig. 44 - Metropolitan Toronto Reference Library;
Fig. 45 - London Public Library;
Fig. 46 - Bowmanville Museum;
Fig. 47 - ibid.;
Fig. 48 - ibid.;
Fig. 49 - Ingersoll Public Library;
Fig. 50 - ibid.;
Fig. 51 - Metropolitan Toronto Reference Library;
Fig. 52 - ibid.;
Fig. 53 - ibid.;
Fig. 54 - Sarnia Public Library;
Fig. 55 - Brad Heintzman;
Fig. 56 - Charles Heintzman;
Fig. 57 - Brad Heintzman;
Fig. 58 - Wendy Thomas;
Fig. 59 - ibid.;
Fig. 60 - Windsor Municipal Archives, MS 6-1/12;
Fig. 61 - *Maclean's*, Paul Rockett photo;
Fig. 62 - Charles Heintzman;
Fig. 63 - Woodstock Public Library;
Fig. 64 - Woodstock Public Archives;
Fig. 65 - ibid.;
Fig. 66 - Caleb Kelly;
Fig. 67 - Woodstock Public Archives;
Fig. 68 - author's photo;
Fig. 69 - ibid.;
Fig. 70 - ibid.;
Fig. 71 - ibid.;
Fig. 72 - ibid.;
Fig. 73 - ibid.;
Fig. 74 - Metropolitan Toronto Reference Library;
Fig. 75 - Listowel Public Archives;
Fig. 76 - ibid.;
Fig. 77 - ibid.;
Fig. 78 - ibid.;
Fig. 79 - Douglas Barber, Patent Office, Ottawa;
Fig. 80 - Metropolitan Toronto Reference Library;
Fig. 81 - ibid.;
Fig. 82 - ibid.;
Fig. 83 - ibid.;
Fig. 84 - London Public Library;
Fig. 85 - R.J. Thompson;
Fig. 86 - author's photo;
Fig. 87 - ibid.;
Fig. 88 - ibid.;
Fig. 89 - Kingston Public Library;
Fig. 90 - ibid.;
Fig. 91 - ibid.;

Fig. 92 - ibid.;
Fig. 93 - ibid.;
Fig. 94 - Robert McLaughlin Gallery [Thomas Bouckley Collection, #0819], Oshawa, Ontario;
Fig. 95 - ibid., #0843;
Fig. 96 - ibid., #0829;
Fig. 97 - ibid., #0813;
Fig. 98 - London Public Library;
Fig. 99 - ibid.;
Fig. 100 - ibid.;
Fig. 101 - author's photo;
Fig. 102 - Waterloo Historical Society;
Fig. 103 - London Public Library;
Fig. 104 - ibid.;
Fig. 105 - New Westminister Public Library;
Fig. 106 - Waterloo Historical Society;
Fig. 107 - Halifax City Regional Library;
Fig. 108 - ibid.;
Fig. 109 - London Public Library;
Fig. 110 - Windsor Public Library;
Fig. 111 - New Westminister Public Library;
Fig. 112 - Douglas Barber, Patent Office, Ottawa;
Fig. 113 - Uxbridge-Scott Historical Society;
Fig. 114 - Barry & Lee Gallerno;
Fig. 115 - ibid.;
Fig. 116 - Woodstock Public Library;
Fig. 117 - Uxbridge-Scott Historical Society;
Fig. 118 - Halifax City Regional Library;
Fig. 119 - Clark Wright;
Fig. 120 - author's photo;
Fig. 121 - ibid.;
Fig. 122 - ibid.;
Fig. 123 - London Public Library;
Fig. 124 - Metropolitan Toronto Reference Library;
Fig. 125 - Douglas Barber, Patent Office, Ottawa;
Fig. 126 - Sociéte Historique de Sainte Thérèse and Léonard Nadeau, Ville de Sainte Thérèse Bibliothéque municipale;
Fig. 127 - Woodstck Public Library;
Fig. 128 - ibid.;
Fig. 129 - Allan Noon;

Page 139 - Norm Amadio;
Page 140 - Photo: Jim Ford & Associates Inc.;
Page 142 - Russell "Bert" Gould;
Page 143 - Russell "Bert" Gould;
Page 144 - Photo: Paul J. Hoeffler;
Page 145 - Anton Kuerti;
Page 146 - Photo courtesy of Al Gilbert, F.R.P.S., Toronto, Canada;
Inside Back Cover - John Arpin;
Back Cover - Charles Heintzman.

ACKNOWLEDGEMENTS

Many individuals and institutions contributed valuable information to this book. Without their help it would not have happened. High on the list of those to whom I am indebted are Murray Draper and Matt Willis. Their recollections of days gone by provided firsthand historical insight that could not have been achieved otherwise.

Also, I would like to thank Douglas Barber, Patent Office, Ottawa; Terry Beer; Bruce and Nadine Bird; Brad Bryden; Andy Burgess; Marjorie Rose Burnett; Derek Chung; Creative Music Studio; Janey Cole, Listowel Public Archives; Barbara Collier; Donald E. Coulman; Debbie Culbert, Printing Unique; Mert Culbert; Glen Curnoe, London Public Library; J.A. Dery; Mrs Gordon Duncan; Bob Ellison; Al Falconer, Huron County Museum; Dwight Fryer; Barry and Lee Gallerno; Fred Haines; Brad Heintzman; Charles Heintzman; Huron County Historical Society; Marg Jackson, Robert McLaughlin Gallery; Linda Kearns, Guelph Public Library; Stewart and Ruth Kelly; John and Marie Kenney; Max Littlejohns; Michael Lipnicki; Mike McDermott; Allan McGillivray, Uxbridge-Scott Historical Society; Dave McKee; Cathy McNeely, *Maclean's*; Edna Meek; Metropolitan Toronto Reference Library; Moir Piano Co. Ltd.; Allan Noon; Murray and Debbie Obre; Bob Pierce; Queen's University Archives; Michael Remenyi; Smithsonian Institution; Guy Sonier; Lynn Stephano; Bryce Stillman; Charles Taws, Bowmanville Museum; Wendy Thomas; Reg Thompson; Ralph Thorn; *Toronto Star*; Gary Trenholm, Doctor Piano Rebuilders; Vivian Warrick; Tim Watcher; Glenn Williams; Woodstock Public Archives; Woodstock Public Library; Clark Wright; Dr Mary Wright; and for their smaller – but no less important – contributions, more than two dozen other public libraries, archives, and historical societies from coast to coast.

I am especially grateful to Barry Penhale and Jane Gibson for their most beneficial suggestions, patience, and encouragement; to the Ontario Heritage Foundation for its kindness and generosity; to Paul Bator of the Foundation for his enthusiasm and helpful guidance; and to my editor, Curtis Fahey.

But most of all, thanks to my wife, Jeannie, and our children, Susan, Sarah, Caleb, Jessica, and Elizabeth, for the writing spells they didn't complain about and for the times when they wisely did.

Wayne Kelly

APPRECIATIONS

The Publisher acknowledges with gratitude the cooperation, recommendations and encouragement provided by the following individuals and organizations.

Russell (Bert) Gould; Ray Roberts; John A. Miller, Cultural Support Services Inc.; Anton Kuerti; Ruth Taylor, Concertmasters Inc.; John Arpin; Norm and Lorraine Amadio; Doreen Davie, Regal Recordings Limited; George Ullmann, Boosey & Hawkes (Canada) Ltd.; Andrew Stewart, Royal Conservatory of Music; Paul Hahn; Bill, Brad and Charles Heintzman; Wendy Thomas; Trevor Owen; Dr. Paul Bator, Ontario Heritage Foundation; Jim Ford, Jim Ford & Associates Inc.; Curtis Fahey; Robin Brass; and Nancy Mayer.

Author, Wayne Kelly and Designer, Derek Chung, are especially deserving of major recognition for their professionalism. Their high work standards are evident throughout the finished publication.

Barry L. Penhale
Publisher

INDEX

Academy (piano), *97*
Alexander, J.W., *52-4*
Alexandra (piano), *97*
Amadio, Norm, *139*
Amherst, NS, *98*
Amherst Piano Co., *97, 111*
Anderson, George, *98*
Appin, ON, *7*
Archambault, Ed, *98*
Arpin, John, *140*
Autonola (piano), *98*

Bagnall Organ & Piano Co., *98-9, 107*
Baker, Nathaniel, *78*
Barclay, Glass & Co., *99*
Barkerville, BC, *19*
Barthelmes, A.A. and F.L., *99*
Beethoven (piano), *30, 93, 99*
Bell (piano), *74*
Bell Piano Co., *31-3, 38, 42-5, 72, 94, 126*
Bell, Robert, *42*
Bell, William, *42-3*
Bell, William Jr., *43*
Bellolian (piano), *99*
Belmont (piano), *99*
Berlin (Kitchener), ON, *23, 99, 106, 114;*
    News Record, 99
Berlin Piano & Organ Co., *99*
Bernhardt, *100*
Best, D.M., *115, 126, 128*
Birch, E., *99*
Birtle Music Club, *19*
Blackburn & Sons, A.R., *100*
Blouin Pianos, Robert, *100*
Blundall Piano Co., *98, 100*
Bohrer, William, *25*
Bord-Favorite (piano), *99*

Bowles, *100*
Bowmanville, ON, *31, 52-3, 97*
Boyd, Thomas, *100*
Brand, Richard Colwell, *29*
Brantford, ON, *45*
Brantford Piano Co., *77, 101*
Breathwaite, Henry, *89*
Brebner, Hubert, *120*
Brebner, James, *58*
Breden, John, Jr., *88*
Broadwood & Sons, *22-3, 101*
Brockley & Co., *98*
Brockley & Misner, *98, 101*
Brockley, Thomas, *101*
Brown, George, *102*
Browne, George, *88*
Bull, Frederick *92*
Burford, ON, *46, 78*
Burrows, Lou, *77*

Calgary, AB, *48, 91*
Canada (piano), *93, 102*
Canada Organ & Piano Co., *91, 102*
Canadian Music Trades Journal, 84
Canadian National Exhibition, *56*
Canadian National Railways, *8, 13*
Canadian Piano Co., *102, 140*
Canadian Patent Office, *27*
Canadian Piano and Organ
    Manufacturers Association, *84*
Cameo (piano), *102*
Carlton (piano), *102*
Carruthers, Betty, *7*
Carruthers, Barbara, *7*
Cecilian Piano Co., *70, 102*
Charbonneau, Louis, *102*
Chase & Baker (piano player), *37, 123*

Chickering (piano), *94*
Chopin (piano), *30, 102*
Chown, C.Y., *89*
Clarke, James P,. *18*
Classic (piano), *102, 128*
Claude & Co., V.W. *102*
Cline, F.C., *88, 102*
Clinton, ON, *12-3, 24, 26, 31, 38, 46-8,*
    84-5, 89, 136, 138
Clinton (piano), *102*
Cluff, D.S., *49*
Colonial Piano Co., *102, 118*
Columbia (piano), *102*
company names, *38*
Concerto (piano), *74, 102*
Concord Canadian (piano), *74, 102*
Continental Euro (piano), *74, 102*
Conner, Thomas, *89*
Consolidated (piano), *103*
Craig (piano), *74*
Craig, David, *103*
Craig Piano Co., *72, 103, 128*
Cross & Co., E. *103*
Crossin & McPhillips, *103*
Crossin & Martens Co., *103*
Cumberland Piano Co., *103*

Daily British Whig, 89
Darley, A.M., *52*
Darley & Robinson, *104*
David & Michaud, *104*
Davis, George, *27*
Dawson, YT, *15*
Denholm (piano), *103*
Dennis, William, *103, 110*
de Pachmann, Vladimir, *65*
Derby (piano), *103*

Diploma (melodeon), *43, 103*
Doherty, William ("W.D."), *28, 31, 46-8, 50*
Doherty Company, W., *12-3, 16, 24, 26, 38, 46-51, 84, 88*
Dolge, Alfred, *18*
Dominion (piano), *103*
Dominion Organ & Piano Co., *31-2, 38, 52-6*
Dowling, J.S., *45*
Draper, Bob, *86*
Draper Bros. & Reid, *86-7, 104*
Draper, Caryl, *50, 85-6*
Draper, Murray, *24, 46, 48*
Dreher, *104*
Drew, Heintzman and Annowski Co., *63*
Ducharme, George, *104*
Duncan, Gordon, *9-10*
Durant, Noah, *104*

Eaton (piano), *104*
T. Eaton Co., *16, 30, 75, 104, 133*
Edmund Piano Co., *104*
Ekfrid Township, *57*
Emerson (piano), *93*
Ennis (piano), *94*
Ennis Piano Co. *32, 104, 111*
Evans Bros. Piano Co., *38, 57-9*
Evans, John, *57*
Evans, William, *57*
Everson (piano), *93, 105*

Farwell Piano Co., *105*
Featherson Piano Co., *105*
Fisher, Edward, *42*
Flaherty, Robert J., *37*
Fletcher, Bill, *15-6*
Foisy, Thomas F.G., *71, 106*
Ford, Clifford, *21, 137*
Foster-Armstrong (piano), *84*
Foster-Armstrong Co., *100, 106*
Fox, Charles F., *88*
Fox, John C., *88*
Fraser & Sons, W., *106*
Friederici, Christian Ernst, *22*
Fuji Piano Co., *31*

Gates Organ & Piano Co., *106*
Gerhard (piano), *106*
Gerhard Heintzman Co., *60-2* (see also Heintzman, Gerhard)
Gibbings, Bert, *85*
Gibson, Joseph, *57*
Glackemeyer, Friedrich, *17*

Glatt, Otta, *28*
Goderich, ON, *133*
Goodwin & Co., Charles, *99, 107*
Gould, Glenn, *142-3*
Gould, Joseph, *25*
Gould, Russell (Bert), *142*
Gourlay-Angelus, *107*
Gourlay, Robert, *75, 107*
Gourlay, Winter & Leeming Co., *15, 31, 75, 84, 107*
Greene, *108*
Grinell Bros., *108-10*
Guelph, ON, *42-3, 72, 111*; *Mercury, 43*

Haddon Hall (piano), *110*
Haines Bros. (piano), *84, 100, 108*
Hale, Joseph P., *30*
Hallett & Davis, *110*
Halifax, NS, *15, 18, 95, 98, 117, 124*
Hamilton, ON, *18, 60, 63, 91, 104-5, 112*
Handel (piano), *110*
Hardy & Sons, *110*
Hargrave, James, *19*
Harmonic (piano), *110*
Harrington (piano), *110*
Hawkins, John Isaac, *23-4*
Haydn Piano Co., *110*
Heintsman-Dalton Co., *110*
Heintzman (piano), *7, 15, 34, 142*
Heintzman & Co., *38, 63-7, 74, 83, 86, 89, 140-1, 145*
Heintzman, Brad, *66*
Heintzman, Charles, *66*
Heintzman, George, *66*
Heintzman, George C., *28, 64*
Heintzman, Gerhard, *60, 107, 112*
Heintzman Piano Company, Gerhard, *60-62*
Heintzman, Matilda, *63*
Heintzman, William (Bill), *66, 86*
Henry Herbert (piano), *110*
Herald, Joseph, *110*
Herbert & Co., J.W., *110*
Hewitt, Daniel, *23*
Hill, Freedom, *25*
Hillcoat Pianos, H.A., *98, 111*
Higel Co., Otto, *37, 40, 126*
Hipkins, A.J., *23*
Hoerr, Franz & Henry, *111*
Hoffman, Dan, *53*
Holly (piano), *111*
Homer (piano), *111*
Hood, Thomas, D., *111*

Hund, Friedrich, *18, 111, 136*
Hund & Seebold, *111*
Hunt, Henry G., *111*
Huron County, *46*

Imperial Piano Co., *111*
Ingersoll, ON, *57, 120*; *Sun, 58*
International Piano Co., *80, 111*

Jackson & Co., *111*
Joiner, Margaret, *7*
Jones & Cross, *111*

Kallmann, Helmut, *19, 114*
Karn (piano), *34, 84*
Karn, Dennis W., *28, 68, 70, 78*
Karn Piano Co., D.W., *31-2, 68-70*
Karn-Warren Co., *69*
Karn-Morris Piano Co., *70, 78*
Kater, Thomas, *111*
Keeso, Charlie, *78*
Kelly, C.W. and J.W., *111*
Kelmonros, *111*
Kennay & Scribner, *112*
Keogh Piano Co., *63*
Kilgour Piano Co., *112*
Kingston, ON, *28, 72, 88-90, 114*
Kitchener, ON, *106*
Knabe (piano), *94*
Knott & Sons, *23, 112*
Kranich & Bach (piano), *112*
Kreisler (piano), *112*
Kuerti, Anton, *144-5*
Krydner (piano), *93, 112*

Labelle & Craig, *103, 112*
Lackner (piano), *112*
Laffargue Piano Co., *112*
Langlier, J. Donat, *112, 117*
Lansdowne Piano Co., *75, 81-2, 112*
Laronda, Laronde, *113*
Laurilliard, *113*
Laverne, *113*
Lawrence Piano Co., *113*
Layton Bros., *113*
Leach, *113*
Leader Pianos, *113*
Leclarion (piano), *113*
Lee, George, *89*
Legare (Royal King), *113*
Leonard, *113*
Lesage, Adélard, *71-2*
Lesage, Demase, *28, 71, 95*
Lesage, Gérard, *72*

Lesage, Isabella, *71*
Lesage, Jacques-Paul, *72*
Lesage, Jules, *72*
Lesage & Fils, *71*
Lesage Pianos Ltd., *31, 45, 71-4, 86, 89-90*
Lesage & Piché, *71*
Leverman & Co., H.A. *113*
Lewis Pianos, *113*
Lighte & Newton Co., *63*
Lindsay Co., C.W., *71, 112-3*
Liszt (piano), *113*
Listowel, ON, *70, 77, 111*; *Banner 77, 79*
Littler, .E.B., *57*
Lodge Pianos, *114*
London, ON, *57, 84, 91, 116*; *Free Press, 19*
London & Sterling (piano), *114*
Lonsdale Piano Co., *114*
Lunn, Frederick, *60*

Maas, J., *23, 114*
McCook, James, *19, 37*
McCarthy, Dennis, *27*
McDonald, J.A., *98*
McDowell, R.J., *89*
McFie, Duncan, *7*
McGee, Timothy, *18*
McGill, Janis, *10*
McGuire, Hillary, *15, 122*
McLaughlin Gallery, Robert, *93*
McManus, James, *88*
McMillan & Co., *114*
McMullan, Richard, *89, 114*
Manby, W.H., *114*
Manning, H.B., *85*
Manning, Wilbur N., *28, 51, 84*
Marcy, Alexander, *26*
Martin, Owain, *114*
Martin-Orme Piano Co., *38*
Marshall & Wendell (piano), *84, 100, 114*
Mason & Risch (piano), *14*
Mason & Risch Piano Co., *30, 37-8, 75-6, 81, 88*
Mason, Henry Herbert, *110*
Mason, Thomas Gabriel, *28, 74, 81-2, 110, 112*
Mead, Mott & Co., *18, 111, 114*
Mechtler (pianoforte instructor), *17*
Mee & Co., *88*
Mehlin & Son, *114*
Mendelssohn (piano), *74, 115-6*
Michaud, Oswald, *115*

Middlesex County, *57*
Miller, Henry F., *115*
Miller & Karn, *68, 121*
Milligan, Francis, *115*
Minuet (piano), *115*
Misner, John, *98, 101*
Mitchell, ON, *9*
Mitchell, J.B., *52-3*
Minx (piano), *85, 115*
Moir, George & William, *115*
Moncton, NB, *95*
Montreal, QC, *15, 17-8, 20, 25-7, 30, 72, 83, 91, 94, 98*
Morris, Feild & Rogers Co., *77-80*
Morris Piano Co., *31, 38, 48, 70, 80, 111*
Mozart Symphony (piano), *31, 115*
Mulholland-Newcombe, *115*
Munro, John, *102*
Music Journal, 19
Muth, William, *115*

National Piano Co., *115*
Nelles, W.B., *57*
Newcombe, Henry, *81*
Newcombe, Octavius, *28, 75, 81-2, 112, 115*
Newcombe Piano Co., *31, 67, 75*
Newmeyer (piano), *99*
New Kauffman (piano), *116*
New Scale Williams (piano) *93*
Nitschke Piano Co., *116*
Nordheimer, Abraham, *28, 82, 112*
Nordheimer, Albert, *75, 82,-3, 112*
Nordheimer, Roy, *83*
Nordheimer, Samuel, *28, 75, 82-3, 112*
Nordheimer Piano Co., *37-8, 75, 82-3, 85*

O'Hara H., *52*
O'Neill Bros., *116*
Ontario Development Corporation, *12*
Ontario Piano Co.,
organ makers index, *131-2*
Orme (see Martin-Orme)
Orme, J.L., *114*
Orth, Charles J., *33*
Oshawa, ON, *52, 54, 91-3*
Oshawa Organ & Melodeon Co., *52, 103, 116*
Oshawa Piano & Cabinet Co., *116*
Ottawa, ON, *95*; *Daily Free Press, 20*
Owen & Son, R.S., *116*
Oxford County, *68*

Palace Grand (piano), *116*
Palmer, T.J., *70*
Palmer Piano Co., *116-7*
Pegg, Addison A., *85-6*
Pense, E.J.B., *89*
Pepin & Sons, *116*
Percival Piano Co., *116*
Perth County, *10*
Peterborough, ON, *29*
Peterson, Oscar, *146-7*
Pfeiffer, J.M., *116*
Philips, H. & J., *101, 106, 117, 124*
Piano and Organ Workers Union, *43*
Pianola (player piano), *39*
Pierce, Bob, *127-8*
Pierce Piano Atlas, *127-8*
Plaola (piano), *93, 117*
Playtona (piano), *117*
Poitras Bros., *117*
Pratte, Louis, *28*
Pratte Piano Co., *117*
Prelude (piano), *74, 117*
Preston, ON, *36, 123*
Preston (piano), *118*
Prince Piano Co., *118*
Princess (piano), *93, 118*
Princess Royal (piano), *118*
Purdy, James, *88*

Quebec, QC, *17-8, 20, 83, 95, 98*; *Gazette, 17*
Quidoz Pianos Ltée, *62, 106, 118*
Quesnel, BC, *19*

Rainer & Co., *118*
Rappe, John, *88, 118*
Red River Academy, *18*
Reed Bros., *118*
Reinhardt, Isaac, *118*
Regina Corona, *70*
Reyner, Joseph, *88, 118*
Reynolds & Duffett, *118*
Richardson, Henry W., *89*
Richardson, Wiliam J., *28*
Risch, Vincent, *28, 75, 81-2, 112*
Robinson & Sons Pianos, *118*
Robinson, William, *52*
Roell, Craig, *16*
Rowe, J.T., *118*
Royal Canadian Legion, *9*
Royal Conservatory of Music, *8, 140*
Royal Ontario Museum, *93, 111*

Saint John, NB, *18, 27, 112-3*

Saint-Saens (piano), *118*
Ste-Thérèse-de-Blainville, QC, *71*, *95*, *118*
Sarnia *Observer*, *63*
Schubert (piano), *30*, *93*, *118*
Schumann (piano), *31*, *74*, *118*
Schumann Piano Co., *118*
Scott, J.W., *77*
Seebold, Manby & Co., *111*, *118*
Seeburg Co., *36*
Seldon T., *57*
Sénécal et Quidoz, *118*
Shaw Co., J.W., *30*, *93*, *99*, *118*
Sherlington (piano), *118*
Sherlock A.E., *85*
Sherlock, Frank J., *16*, *28*, *51*, *84*
Sherlock, G.W., *85*
Sherlock-Manning Piano Co., *12-3*, *16*, *24*, *38*, *40-1*, *46*, *51*, *70*, *74*, *84-7*, *89-90*, *136*
Slade B., *118*
Small, Charles Wassan, *100*
Small & McArthur, *101*, *118*
Smith, Alexander, *120*
Smith, A.M., *26*
Smith, F.G. (piano), *118*
Snyder & Co., W.H., *100*, *118*
Solo Player Piano Co., *119*
Sonata (piano), *74*, *119*
Sonobel (piano), *119*
Soper, Lewis N., *119*
Sovereign, *119*
Standard Piano Co., *119*
Stanley Piano Co., *31*, *111*, *119-20*
Steinbach (piano), *120*
Steinway, Henry, *63*
Steinway & Sons, *30*, *65*, *94*
Stellarton, NS, *94*
Stephenson, John, *120*
Sterling Action & Keys Co., *70*
Sterling (piano), *120*
Stevenson, John and W.H., *88*
Stevenson & Co., *88*, *120*
Stodart, William, *22*, *101*

Strathmore (piano), *120*
Sumner, Ernest, *58*
Sumner, Sidney, *58*
Sumner & Brebner Piano Co., *38*, *120*
Sullivan, Sir Arthur, *81*

Thomas Organ & Piano Co., C.L., *120*
Thomas Organ & Piano Co., *120-22*
Thomas, Charles L., *63*, *120-1*
Thomas, Edward G., *120-1*
Thomas, Frank J., *63*, *122*
Thomas, John Morgan, *120*
Thomas, John L., *122*
Thomas, Thomas L., *122*
Thornton, E.C., *77*
Townsend, William, *91*
Toronto, ON, *16*, *18*, *20*, *28*, *37*, *60*, *65*, *69*, *70*, *75*, *82*, *86*, *91*, *98*, *100*; *Globe*, *38-9*, *54*, *62*, *83*, *101*; *Mail*, *58*, *69*
Toronto Conservatory of Music, *42*
Toronto Normal School, *18*
Trois-Rivières, *95*
Tudhope, W.R., *78*

United Empire Loyalists, *20*
Uxbridge, ON, *15*, *100*, *116*, *142*
Uxbridge Piano Co., *100-01*, *122*

Vancouver, BC, *15-16*, *64*, *98*, *105*
Van Rohl, Paul, *119*
Versailles (piano), *74*, *122*
Victoria, BC, *15*, *19*; *British Colonist*, *107*
Victoria (Queen), *43*, *64*, *81*
vorsetzer (piano player), *36*

Wadsworth (piano), *123*
Wagner, Zeidler & Co., *123*
Walls, Prince & Wilks, *118*, *123*
Watterworth, Kenneth, *58*
Watterworth, William, *57-8*
Warren Co., S.R., *69*, *123*
Weber (piano), *74*
Weber, George M., *88*
Weber Piano Co., *72*, *88-90*

Werlich Bros. Co., *36*, *123-4*
Western Piano Manufactory, *63*, *124*
Westmount, QC, *26*
Whaley-Royce Piano Co., *31-2*, *124*
White, Charles, *58*
White, David, *57*
Williams (piano), *93*
Williams Piano Co., R.S., *38*, *54*, *89*, *91-4*
Williams, Richard Sugden, *91*
Williams, Richard Sugden, Jr., *92*
Williams, Robert, *92*
Williams & Leverman, *124-5*
Willis, Albert, *81*
Willis, Alexander ("A.P."), *28*, *94*
Willis, Austin, *95*
Willis, Frank, *95*
Willis, Inglis, *95*
Willis, John James, *94*
Willis, Matthew, *27*, *32*, *76*, *95-6*, *113*
Willis, Nathaniel Parker, *94*
Willis Piano Co., *27*, *37-8*, *54*, *71*, *74*, *76*, *86*, *94-6*
Willis, Robert, *94*
Willis & Baker, *125*
Wilson, H.C. (piano), *125*
Windsor, ON, *66-7*, *108-10*
Winnipeg, MB, *16*, *18-9*, *48*, *83*, *91*
Winnipeg Piano Co., *125*
Winter & Co., *75-6*
Woodstock, ON, *31*, *68-70*, *78*, *126*; *Evening Sentinel-Review*, *68-9*, *121*; Organ Co., *70*; Pipe Organ Builders, *70*
Wornum, Robert, *23*
Wormwith Piano Co., *88-90*
Wormwith, W.H., *89*
Wright Piano Co., *125*
Wurlitzer Co., *36*

Yamaha Music Company, *25*, *31*
Yates George, *48*
York Factory, MB, *19*